M000205421

HBR'S 10 MUST READS

On
Leadership
Lessons
from Sports

HBR's 10 Must Reads series is the definitive collection of ideas and best practices for aspiring and experienced leaders alike. These books offer essential reading selected from the pages of *Harvard Business Review* on topics critical to the success of every manager.

Titles include:

HBR's 10 Must Reads 2015
HBR's 10 Must Reads 2016
HBR's 10 Must Reads 2017
HBR's 10 Must Reads 2018
HBR's 10 Must Reads for New Managers
HBR's 10 Must Reads on Change Management
HBR's 10 Must Reads on Collaboration
HBR's 10 Must Reads on Communication
HBR's 10 Must Reads on Emotional Intelligence
HBR's 10 Must Reads on Entrepreneurship and Startups
HBR's 10 Must Reads on Innovation
HBR's 10 Must Reads on Leadership
HBR's 10 Must Reads on Leadership Lessons from Sports
HBR's 10 Must Reads on Making Smart Decisions
HBR's 10 Must Reads on Managing Across Cultures
HBR's 10 Must Reads on Managing People
HBR's 10 Must Reads on Managing Yourself
HBR's 10 Must Reads on Mental Toughness
HBR's 10 Must Reads on Sales
HBR's 10 Must Reads on Strategic Marketing
HBR's 10 Must Reads on Strategy
HBR's 10 Must Reads on Teams
HBR's 10 Must Reads: The Essentials

On
Leadership
Lessons
from Sports

HARVARD BUSINESS REVIEW PRESS
Boston, Massachusetts

HBR Press Quantity Sales Discounts

Harvard Business Review Press titles are available at significant quantity discounts when purchased in bulk for client gifts, sales promotions, and premiums. Special editions, including books with corporate logos, customized covers, and letters from the company or CEO printed in the front matter, as well as excerpts of existing books, can also be created in large quantities for special needs.

For details and discount information for both print and ebook formats, contact booksales@harvardbusiness.org, tel 800-988-0886, or www.hbr.org/bulksales.

Copyright 2018 Harvard Business School Publishing Corporation
All rights reserved
Printed in the United States of America
10 9 8 7 6 5 4 3 2 1

No part of this publication may be reproduced, stored in or introduced into a retrieval system, or transmitted, in any form, or by any means (electronic, mechanical, photocopying, recording, or otherwise), without the prior permission of the publisher. Requests for permission should be directed to permissions@hbsp.harvard.edu, or mailed to Permissions, Harvard Business School Publishing, 60 Harvard Way, Boston, Massachusetts 02163.

The web addresses referenced in this book were live and correct at the time of the book's publication but may be subject to change.

Library of Congress Cataloging-in-Publication Data
Title: HBR's 10 must reads on leadership lessons from sports.
Other titles: Harvard Business Review's ten must reads on leadership lessons from sports | HBR's 10 must reads (Series)
Description: Boston, Massachusetts : Harvard Business Review Press, [2018] | Series: HBR's 10 must reads (Series)
Identifiers: LCCN 2017034847 | ISBN 9781633694347 (pbk. : alk. paper)
Subjects: LCSH: Leadership. | Success in business. | Athletes—Psychology.
Classification: LCC HD57.7 .H3915 2018 | DDC 658.4/092—dc23 LC record available at https://lccn.loc.gov/2017034847

The paper used in this publication meets the requirements of the American National Standard for Permanence of Paper for Publications and Documents in Libraries and Archives Z39.48-1992.

ISBN: 9781633694347
eISBN: 9781633694354

Contents

HBR'S
10
MUST
READS

On
**Leadership
Lessons
from Sports**

Ferguson's Formula

by Anita Elberse with Sir Alex Ferguson

SOME CALL HIM THE GREATEST COACH IN HISTORY. Before retiring in May 2013, Sir Alex Ferguson spent 26 seasons as the manager of Manchester United, the English football (soccer) club that ranks among the most successful and valuable franchises in sports. During that time the club won 13 English league titles along with 25 other domestic and international trophies—giving him an overall haul nearly double that of the next-most-successful English club manager. And Ferguson was far more than a coach. He played a central role in the United organization, managing not just the first team but the entire club. "Steve Jobs was Apple; Sir Alex Ferguson is Manchester United," says the club's former chief executive David Gill.

In 2012 Harvard Business School professor Anita Elberse had a unique opportunity to examine Ferguson's management approach and developed an HBS case study around it. Now she and Ferguson have collaborated on an analysis of his enormously successful methods.

Anita Elberse: Success and staying power like Sir Alex Ferguson's demand study—and not just by football fans. How did he do it? Can one identify habits that enabled his success and principles that guided it? During what turned out to be his final season in charge, my former student Tom Dye and I conducted a series of in-depth interviews with Ferguson about his leadership methods and watched him in action at United's training ground and at its famed stadium, Old Trafford, where a nine-foot bronze statue of the former manager now looms outside. We spoke with many of the people Ferguson worked with, from David Gill to the club's assistant coaches, kit manager, and players. And we observed Ferguson during numerous short meetings and conversations with players and staff members in the hallways, in the cafeteria, on the training pitch, and wherever else the opportunity arose. Ferguson later came to HBS to see the ensuing case study taught, provide his views, and answer students' questions, resulting in standing-room-only conditions in my classroom and a highly captivating exchange.

Ferguson and I discussed eight leadership lessons that capture crucial elements of his approach. Although I've tried not to push the angle *too* hard, many of them can certainly be applied more broadly, to business and to life. In the article that follows, I describe each lesson as I observed it, and then give Ferguson his say.

Start with the Foundation

Upon his arrival at Manchester, in 1986, Ferguson set about creating a structure for the long term by modernizing United's youth program. He established two "centers of excellence" for promising players as young as nine and recruited a number of scouts, urging them to bring him the top young talent. The best-known of his early signings was David Beckham. The most important was probably Ryan Giggs, whom Ferguson noticed as a skinny 13-year-old in 1986 and who went on to become the most decorated British footballer of all time. At 39, Giggs is still a United regular. The longtime stars Paul Scholes and Gary Neville were also among Ferguson's early youth program investments. Together with Giggs and Beckham, they formed the core of the great United teams of the late 1990s and early 2000s, which Ferguson credits with shaping the club's modern identity.

It was a big bet on young talent, and at a time when the prevailing wisdom was, as one respected television commentator put it, "You can't win anything with kids." Ferguson approached the process

Idea in Brief

The Record

Before his retirement in May 2013, after 26 years in charge at the English football club Manchester United, Sir Alex Ferguson was perhaps the most successful coach in all of sports. United won the English league 13 times during his tenure, along with 25 other domestic and international trophies.

The Question

What were the methods behind Ferguson's success, and can they be applied beyond the playing field?

The Lessons

Ferguson's approach can be broken down into eight leadership principles, ranging from the value of standing back and observing to the specifics of preparing to win.

systematically. He talks about the difference between building a team, which is what most managers concentrate on, and building a club.

Sir Alex Ferguson: From the moment I got to Manchester United, I thought of only one thing: building a football club. I wanted to build right from the bottom. That was in order to create fluency and a continuity of supply to the first team. With this approach, the players all grow up together, producing a bond that, in turn, creates a spirit.

When I arrived, only one player on the first team was under 24. Can you imagine that, for a club like Manchester United? I knew that a focus on youth would fit the club's history, and my earlier coaching experience told me that winning with young players could be done and that I was good at working with them. So I had the confidence and conviction that if United was going to mean anything again, rebuilding the youth structure was crucial. You could say it was brave, but fortune favors the brave.

The first thought of 99% of newly appointed managers is to make sure they win—to survive. So they bring experienced players in.

That's simply because we're in a results-driven industry. At some clubs, you need only to lose three games in a row, and you're fired. In today's football world, with a new breed of directors and owners, I am not sure any club would have the patience to wait for a manager to build a team over a four-year period.

Winning a game is only a short-term gain—you can lose the next game. Building a club brings stability and consistency. You don't ever want to take your eyes off the first team, but our youth development efforts ended up leading to our many successes in the 1990s and early 2000s. The young players really became the spirit of the club.

I always take great pride in seeing younger players develop. The job of a manager, like that of a teacher, is to inspire people to be better. Give them better technical skills, make them winners, make them better people, and they can go anywhere in life. When you give young people a chance, you not only create a longer life span for the team, you also create loyalty. They will always remember that you were the manager who gave them their first opportunity. Once they know you are batting for them, they will accept your way. You're really fostering a sense of family. If you give young people your attention and an opportunity to succeed, it is amazing how much they will surprise you.

Dare to Rebuild Your Team

Even in times of great success, Ferguson worked to rebuild his team. He is credited with assembling five distinct league-winning squads during his time at the club and continuing to win trophies all the while. His decisions were driven by a keen sense of where his team stood in the cycle of rebuilding and by a similarly keen sense of players' life cycles—how much value the players were bringing to the team at any point in time. Managing the talent development process inevitably involved cutting players, including loyal veterans to whom Ferguson had a personal attachment. "He's never really looking at this moment, he's always looking into the future," Ryan Giggs told us. "Knowing what needs strengthening and what needs refreshing—he's got that knack."

Our analysis of a decade's worth of player transfer data revealed Ferguson to be a uniquely effective "portfolio manager" of talent. He is strategic, rational, and systematic. In the past decade, during which Manchester United won the English league five times, the club spent less on incoming transfers than its rivals Chelsea, Manchester City, and Liverpool did. One reason was a continued commitment to young players: Those under 25 constituted a far higher share of United's incoming transfers than of its competitors'. And because United was willing to sell players who still had good years ahead of them, it made more money from outgoing transfers than most of its rivals did—so the betting on promising talent could continue. Many of those bets were made on very young players on the cusp of superstardom. (Ferguson did occasionally shell out top money for established superstars, such as the Dutch striker Robin van Persie, bought for $35 million at the start of the 2012–2013 season, when he was 29.) Young players were given the time and conditions to succeed, most older players were sold to other teams while they were still valuable properties, and a few top veterans were kept around to lend continuity and carry the culture of the club forward.

Ferguson: We identified three levels of players: those 30 and older, those roughly 23 to 30, and the younger ones coming in. The idea was that the younger players were developing and would meet the standards that the older ones had set. Although I was always trying to disprove it, I believe that the cycle of a successful team lasts maybe four years, and then some change is needed. So we tried to visualize the team three or four years ahead and make decisions accordingly. Because I was at United for such a long time, I could afford to plan ahead—no one expected me to go anywhere. I was very fortunate in that respect.

The goal was to evolve gradually, moving older players out and younger players in. It was mainly about two things: First, who did we have coming through and where did we see them in three years' time, and second, were there signs that existing players were getting older? Some players can go on for a long time, like Ryan Giggs, Paul Scholes, and Rio Ferdinand, but age matters. The hardest thing is to let go of a player who has been a great guy—but all the evidence is on the field. If you see the change, the deterioration, you have to ask yourself what things are going to be like two years ahead.

Set High Standards—and Hold Everyone to Them

Ferguson speaks passionately about wanting to instill values in his players. More than giving them technical skills, he wanted to inspire them to strive to do better and to never give up—in other words, to make them winners.

His intense desire to win stemmed in part from his own experiences as a player. After success at several small Scottish clubs, he signed with a top club, Rangers—the team he had supported as a boy—but soon fell out of favor with the new manager. He left Rangers three years later with only a Scottish Cup Final runner-up's medal to show for his time there. "The adversity gave me a sense of determination that has shaped my life," he told us. "I made up my mind that I would never give in."

Ferguson looked for the same attitude in his players. He recruited what he calls "bad losers" and demanded that they work extremely hard. Over the years this attitude became contagious—players didn't accept teammates' *not* giving it their all. The biggest stars were no exception.

Ferguson: Everything we did was about maintaining the standards we had set as a football club—this applied to all my team building and all my team preparation, motivational talks, and tactical talks. For example, we never allowed a bad training session. What you see in training manifests itself on the game field. So every training session was about quality. We didn't allow a lack of focus. It was about intensity, concentration, speed—a high level of performance. That, we hoped, made our players improve with each session.

I had to lift players' expectations. They should never give in. I said that to them all the time: "If you give in once, you'll give in twice." And the work ethic and energy I had seemed to spread throughout the club. I used to be the first to arrive in the morning. In my later years, a lot of my staff members would already be there when I got in at 7 a.m. I think they understood why I came in early—they knew there was a job to be done. There was a feeling that "if he can do it, then I can do it."

I constantly told my squad that working hard all your life is a talent. But I expected even more from the star players. I expected them to work even harder. I said, "You've got to show that you are the top players." And they did. That's *why* they are star players—they are prepared to work harder. Superstars with egos are not the problem some people may think. They need to be winners, because that massages their egos, so they will do what it takes to win. I used to see [Cristiano] Ronaldo [one of the world's top forwards, who now plays for Real Madrid], Beckham, Giggs, Scholes, and others out there practicing for hours. I'd have to chase them in. I'd be banging on the window saying, "We've got a game on Saturday." But they wanted the time to practice. They realized that being a Manchester United player is not an easy job.

Never, Ever Cede Control

"You can't ever lose control—not when you are dealing with 30 top professionals who are all millionaires," Ferguson told us. "And if any players want to take me on, to challenge my authority and control, I deal with them." An important part of maintaining high standards across the board was Ferguson's willingness to respond forcefully when players violated those standards. If they got into trouble, they were fined. And if they stepped out of line in a way that could undermine the team's performance, Ferguson let them go. In 2005, when longtime captain Roy Keane publicly criticized his teammates, his contract was terminated. The following year, when United's leading scorer at the time, Ruud van Nistelrooy, became openly disgruntled over several benchings, he was promptly sold to Real Madrid.

Responding forcefully is only part of the story here. Responding quickly, before situations get out of hand, may be equally important to maintaining control.

Ferguson: If the day came that the manager of Manchester United was controlled by the players—in other words, if the players decided how the training should be, what days they should have off, what the discipline should be, and what the tactics should be—then Manchester United would not be the Manchester United we know. Before I came to United, I told myself I wasn't going to allow anyone to be stronger than I was. Your personality has to be bigger than theirs. That is vital.

There are occasions when you have to ask yourself whether certain players are affecting the dressing-room atmosphere, the performance of the team, and your control of the players and staff. If they are, you have to cut the cord. There is absolutely no other way. It doesn't matter if the person is the best player in the world. The long-term view of the club is more important than any individual, and the manager has to be the most important one in the club.

Some English clubs have changed managers so many times that it creates power for the players in the dressing room. That is very dangerous. If the coach has no control, he will not last. You have to achieve a position of comprehensive control. Players must recognize that as the manager, you have the status to control events. You can complicate your life in many ways by asking, "Oh, I wonder if the players like me?" If I did my job well, the players would respect me, and that's all you need.

I tended to act quickly when I saw a player become a negative influence. Some might say I acted impulsively, but I think it was critical that I made up my mind quickly. Why should I have gone to bed with doubts? I would wake up the next day and take the necessary steps to maintain discipline. It's important to have confidence in yourself to make a decision and to move on once you have. It's not about looking for adversity or for opportunities to prove power; it's about having control and being authoritative when issues do arise.

Match the Message to the Moment

When it came to communicating decisions to his players, Ferguson—perhaps surprisingly for a manager with a reputation for being tough and demanding—worked hard to tailor his words to the situation.

When he had to tell a player who might have been expecting to start that he wouldn't be starting, he would approach it as a delicate assignment. "I do it privately," he told us. "It's not easy. I say, 'Look, I might be making a mistake here'—I always say that—'but I think this is the best team for today.' I try to give them a bit of confidence, telling them that it is only tactical and that bigger games are coming up."

During training sessions in the run-up to games, Ferguson and his assistant coaches emphasized the positives. And although the media often portrayed him as favoring ferocious halftime and postgame talks, in fact he varied his approach. "You can't always come in shouting and screaming," he told us. "That doesn't work." The former player Andy Cole described it this way: "If you lose and Sir Alex believes you gave your best, it's not a problem. But if you lose [in a] limp way . . . then mind your ears!"

Ferguson: No one likes to be criticized. Few people get better with criticism; most respond to encouragement instead. So I tried to give encouragement when I could. For a player—for any human being—there is nothing better than hearing "Well done." Those are the two best words ever invented. You don't need to use superlatives.

At the same time, in the dressing room, you need to point out mistakes when players don't meet expectations. That is when reprimands are important. I would do it right after the game. I wouldn't wait until Monday. I'd do it, and it was finished. I was on to the next match. There is no point in criticizing a player forever.

Generally, my pregame talks were about our expectations, the players' belief in themselves, and their trust in one another. I liked to refer to a working-class principle. Not all players come from a working-class background, but maybe their fathers do, or their grandfathers, and I found it useful to remind players how far they have come. I would tell them that having a work ethic is very important. It seemed to enhance their pride. I would remind them that it is trust in one another, not letting their mates down, that helps build the character of a team.

In halftime talks, you have maybe eight minutes to deliver your message, so it is vital to use the time well. Everything is easier

Journey to Greatness

November 6, 1986

Alex Ferguson is named manager of Manchester United, having won 10 major trophies in six years at Aberdeen, including a European cup over Real Madrid. United is second to last in its league and faces the threat of being relegated to a lower division. But under Ferguson's leadership, it finishes the season 11th out of 22 teams.

May 12, 1990

Manchester United wins its first trophy under Ferguson—the prestigious FA (Football Association) Cup. His United teams will ultimately win 38 domestic and international titles, making Ferguson the most decorated manager in English football history.

March 2, 1991

Ryan Giggs makes his league debut. Giggs, then 17, came up through the club's youth academy, which Ferguson revitalized upon his arrival. Giggs is widely recognized as one of the most influential players in the club's 135-year history, having made a record number of appearances and won an unmatched 35 trophies to date.

June 7, 1991

Chairman Martin Edwards floats Manchester United on the London Stock Exchange. When the club goes public, it is valued at £47 million. The IPO raises £6.7 million.

May 2, 1993

Manchester United wins the Premier League, formed at the close of the previous season by the 22 clubs in the Football League First Division. It is United's first league title in 26 years. The club will win the Premier League 12 more times during Ferguson's tenure.

September 10, 1998

The subscription network MUTV is launched, airing sports talk shows, Q&As with club staff members and players, and replays of games. As of 2013 it is offered in 57 countries and brings United almost £9 million in annual revenue.

August 1998–May 1999

Manchester United wins the Treble: the Premier League, the FA Cup, and the UEFA (Union of European Football Associations) Champions League title. It is the only English team ever to have achieved this feat. Alex Ferguson soon becomes Sir Alex Ferguson, knighted for his service to the sport. Global support for United soars.

April 14, 2001

Ferguson becomes the first manager since the inception of the English league, in 1888, to win the title in three consecutive years. He will repeat this achievement in 2009.

August 1, 2002

A 13-year kit sponsorship deal with Nike goes into effect. Worth £23.3 million a year, it is the largest uniform contract in English football at that time.

August 12, 2003

The club acquires Cristiano Ronaldo from Sporting Lisbon for £12.2 million. Six years later United sells the Portuguese forward to Real Madrid for £80 million, a record-breaking sum.

May 16, 2005

The U.S. sports team owner Malcolm Glazer acquires a controlling interest in the club and soon delists it from the London exchange. Trades totaling nearly £800 million later give the Glazer family sole ownership. During United's 14 years as a public company, the club's value increased almost 17-fold.

August 18, 2008

Saudi Telecom signs a five-year deal with United, giving it access to video highlights and other content for mobile phones. Commercial revenue will play an increasing role in the club's finances, contributing £118 million in the 2012 fiscal year and rising 28% in the first three quarters of fiscal 2013.

August 10, 2012

The Glazer family floats Manchester United on the New York Stock Exchange. The club's worth is listed at $2.3 billion, making United the most valuable sports franchise in the world.

May 8, 2013

Ferguson retires from Manchester United. During his last season, the club wins its 20th English league title, giving it the most of any team. It has annual revenue of more than £320 million, representing a 13-fold increase in the 20 years since Ferguson's first league title.

when you are winning: You can talk about concentrating, not getting complacent, and the small things you can address. But when you are losing, you have to make an impact. I liked to focus on our own team and our own strengths, but you have to correct why you are losing.

In our training sessions, we tried to build a football team with superb athletes who were smart tactically. If you are too soft in your approach, you won't be able to achieve that. Fear has to come into it. But you can be *too* hard; if players are fearful all the time, they won't perform well either. As I've gotten older, I've come to see that showing your anger all the time doesn't work. You have to pick your moments. As a manager, you play different roles at different times. Sometimes you have to be a doctor, or a teacher, or a father.

Prepare to Win

Ferguson's teams had a knack for pulling out victories in the late stages of games. Our analysis of game results shows that over 10 recent seasons, United had a better record when tied at halftime and when tied with 15 minutes left to play than any other club in the English league. Inspirational halftime talks and the right tactical changes during the game undoubtedly had something to do with those wins, but they may not be the full story.

When their teams are behind late in the game, many managers will direct players to move forward, encouraging them to attack. Ferguson was both unusually aggressive and unusually systematic about his approach. He *prepared* his team to win. He had players regularly practice how they should play if a goal was needed with 10, five, or three minutes remaining. "We practice for when the going gets tough, so we know what it takes to be successful in those situations," one of United's assistant coaches told us.

United practice sessions focused on repetition of skills and tactics. "We look at the training sessions as opportunities to learn and improve," Ferguson said. "Sometimes the players might think, 'Here we go again,' but it helps us win." There appears to be more to this approach than just the common belief that winning teams are rooted in habits—that they can execute certain plays almost automatically. There is also an underlying signal that you are never quite satisfied with where you are and are constantly looking for ways to improve. This is how Ferguson put it: "The message is simple: We cannot sit still at this club."

Ferguson: Winning is in my nature. I've set my standards over such a long period of time that there is no other option for me—I *have* to win. I expected to win every time we went out there. Even if five of the most important players were injured, I expected to win. Other teams get into a huddle before the start of a match, but I did not do that with my team. Once we stepped onto the pitch before a game, I was confident that the players were prepared and ready to play, because everything had been done before they walked out onto the pitch.

I am a gambler—a risk taker—and you can see that in how we played in the late stages of matches. If we were down at halftime, the message was simple: Don't panic. Just concentrate on getting the task done. If we were still down—say, 1-2—with 15 minutes to go, I was ready to take more risks. I was perfectly happy to lose 1-3 if it meant we'd given ourselves a good chance to draw or to win. So in those last 15 minutes, we'd go for it. We'd put in an extra attacking player and worry less about defense. We knew that if we ended up winning 3-2, it would be a fantastic feeling. And if we lost 1-3, we'd been losing anyway.

Being positive and adventurous and taking risks—that was our style. We were there to win the game. Our supporters understood that, and they got behind it. It was a wonderful feeling, you know, to see us go for it in those last 15 minutes. A bombardment in the box, bodies everywhere, players putting up a real fight. Of course, you can lose on the counterattack, but the joy of winning when you thought you were beaten is fantastic.

I think all my teams had perseverance—they never gave in. So I didn't really need to worry about getting that message across. It's a fantastic characteristic to have, and it is amazing to see what can happen in the dying seconds of a match.

Rely on the Power of Observation

Ferguson started out as a manager at the small Scottish club East Stirlingshire in 1974, when he was 32. He was not much older than some of his players and was very hands-on. As he moved up—to St. Mirren and Aberdeen, in Scotland, and then, after spectacular success at Aberdeen, to Manchester United—he increasingly delegated the training sessions to his assistant coaches. But he was always present, and he *watched*. The switch from coaching to observing, he told us, allowed him to better evaluate the players and their performances. "As a coach on the field, you don't see everything," he noted. A regular observer, however, can spot changes in training patterns, energy levels, and work rates.

The key is to delegate the direct supervision to others and trust them to do their jobs, allowing the manager to truly observe.

Ferguson: Observation is the final part of my management structure. When I started as a coach, I relied on several basics: that I could play the game well, that I understood the technical skills needed to succeed at the highest level, that I could coach players, and that I had the ability to make decisions. One afternoon at Aberdeen I had a conversation with my assistant manager while we were having a cup of tea. He said, "I don't know why you brought me here." I said, "What are you talking about?" and he replied, "I don't *do* anything. I work with the youth team, but I'm here to assist you with the training and with picking the team. That's the assistant manager's job." And another coach said, "I think he's right, boss," and pointed out that I could benefit from not always having to lead the training. At first I said, "No, no, no," but I thought it over for a few days and then said, "I'll give it a try. No promises." Deep down I knew he was right. So I delegated the training to him, and it was the best thing I ever did.

It didn't take away my control. My presence and ability to supervise were always there, and what you can pick up by watching is incredibly valuable. Once I stepped out of the bubble, I became more aware of a range of details, and my performance level jumped. Seeing a change in a player's habits or a sudden dip in his enthusiasm allowed me to go further with him: Is it family problems? Is he struggling financially? Is he tired? What kind of mood is he in? Sometimes I could even tell that a player was injured when he thought he was fine.

I don't think many people fully understand the value of observing. I came to see observation as a critical part of my management skills. The ability to see things is key—or, more specifically, the ability to see things you don't expect to see.

Never Stop Adapting

In Ferguson's quarter of a century at United, the world of football changed dramatically, from the financial stakes involved (with both positive and negative consequences) to the science behind what makes players better. Responding to change is never easy, and it is perhaps even harder when one is on top for so long. Yet evidence of Ferguson's willingness to change is everywhere. As David Gill described it to me, Ferguson has "demonstrated a tremendous capacity to adapt as the game has changed."

In the mid-1990s, Ferguson became the first manager to field teams with a large number of young players in the relatively unprestigious League Cup—a practice that initially caused outrage but now is common among Premier League clubs (the Premier League consists of the country's top 20 teams). He was also the first to let four top center forwards spend a season battling for two positions on his roster, a strategy that many outsiders deemed unmanageable but that was key to the great 1998–1999 season, in which United won the Treble: the Premier League, the FA (Football Association) Cup, and the UEFA (Union of European Football Associations) Champions League.

Off the field, Ferguson greatly expanded his back-room staff and appointed a team of sports scientists to support the coaches. Following their suggestions, he installed Vitamin D booths in the players' dressing room in order to compensate for the lack of sunlight in Manchester, and championed the use of vests fitted with GPS sensors that allow an analysis of performance just 20 minutes after a training session. Ferguson was the first coach to employ an optometrist for his players. United also hired a yoga instructor to work with players twice a week and recently unveiled a state-of-the-art medical facility at its training ground so that all procedures short of surgery can be handled on-site—ensuring a level of discretion impossible in a public hospital, where details about a player's condition are invariably leaked to the press.

Ferguson: When I started, there were no agents, and although games were televised, the media did not elevate players to the level of film stars and constantly look for new stories about them. Stadiums have improved, pitches are in perfect condition now, and sports science has a strong influence on how we prepare for the season. Owners from Russia, the Middle East, and other regions have poured a lot of money into the game and are putting pressure on managers. And players have led more-sheltered lives, so they are much more fragile than players were 25 years ago.

One of the things I've done well over the years is manage change. I believe that you control change by accepting it. That also means having confidence in the people you hire. The minute staff members are employed, you have to trust that they are doing their jobs. If you micromanage and tell people what to do, there is no point in hiring them. The most important thing is to not stagnate. I said to David Gill a few years ago, "The only way we can keep players at Manchester United is if we have the best training ground in Europe." That is when we kick-started the medical center. We can't sit still.

Most people with my kind of track record don't look to change. But I always felt I couldn't afford *not* to change. We had to be successful—there was no other option for me—and I would explore any means of improving. I continued to work hard. I treated every success as my first. My job was to give us the best possible chance of winning. That is what drove me.

Originally published in October 2013. Reprint R1310G

An Interview with Greg Louganis

Greg Louganis *dominated world diving competitions in the 1980s, scoring double gold medals in back-to-back Olympic Games. But a more meaningful triumph came years later, when he revealed to the public that he was both gay and HIV-positive and became an advocate for human rights. He now mentors top U.S. divers.* **Interviewed by Alison Beard**

HBR: *Why did you gravitate to an individual sport?*

Louganis: It was a progression. I started dance and acrobatics when I was one and a half and performing onstage when I was three. I got a partner, and we had to wait until we were six to compete, but once we did, we started winning everything. She went into gymnastics, and I followed her, and it was my love; I wanted to make the Olympic team. But outside San Diego, where I grew up, there wasn't a strong men's team. When I was about eight, we had a pool built in our backyard, so I started trying some of my gymnastic stunts off the diving board. My mom didn't want me to kill myself, so she got me lessons. After a year, the coach asked if I would join the club team, and that's how it all started. I wasn't interested in competition. I was interested in performing. I don't really view myself as a competitor.

That's an interesting thing for an Olympian to say. What do you see as the difference between the two?

In competition, you're looking at a supposed rival and trying to beat them. I was more interested in how far I could push myself.

And how did you do that?

My body—measurements, muscle composition—I was blessed with that. The rest was hard work: getting in the pool, rain or shine, putting the hours in. I always traveled with a Speedo in my bag because I never knew when I'd have the opportunity to get on the boards and train.

You're known for your focus. How did you mentally prepare for competition?

I learned visualization at age three. Before my first performance, we had tech and dress rehearsals—I wore a little tux with a top hat and cane—but my teacher knew that if I had to do the routine over and over, I would be too fatigued to perform that night. So she put me in the studio, played the music, and said, "Imagine yourself doing the routine." It took four times before it was completely fluid, without a hitch or hesitation, and then she turned up the tempo and said, "Do it again." I did, and when I performed that night, I didn't miss a step. So I took that tool into everything that I did: dance, gymnastics, diving. That's how I prepared.

You famously hit your head during a dive in the 1988 Games in Seoul but came back to win gold. How did you push through?

To get over something like that—to process, understand, analyze—takes time. I had 22 minutes until my next dive. My coach, Ron O'Brien, said, "You don't have to go back. You have an incredible record. Whatever you decide, I'm behind you 100%." But my knee-jerk reaction was: "We worked too long and hard to get here. I don't want to give up without a fight." So he said, "You know, hockey players get 30 stitches and get back on the ice. You got five." We started laughing. Then he said, "Look, Greg, this was a total fluke. So get up there like it never happened. If you don't believe in yourself, believe in me, because I believe in you." That's how I was able to get back up on the board. It's not that I got over it. I just set it aside like it never existed.

We know now that you were also HIV-positive at the time and were worried that your blood might infect others. How much did that influence your thinking?

My first feeling was embarrassment: *How do I get out of this pool without anybody seeing me?* Then I got angry with myself. And then there was the realization: *God, what is my responsibility?* I was in a country that, had officials known my HIV status, wouldn't have allowed me in. And so, like I said in my book, I was paralyzed by fear. But the one thing I knew was diving. So that's what I focused on.

You won your first Olympic medal—silver—at age 16. How did you respond to the fame that came with that win?

That was an odd period. I was a sophomore in high school. My coach was Dr. Sammy Lee, who won two Olympic gold medals, in '48 and '52, and coached Bobby Webster to do the same, in '60 and '64. In 1976 Klaus Dibiasi was going for his third Olympic gold medal, and I felt that my sole purpose on earth was to prevent him from breaking my coach's record. And so, in my mind's eye, I failed, because I went there to win. I didn't go there to take second.

But you were being celebrated.

That was what was so confusing: Why were they celebrating my failure? The kids that bullied me growing up all of a sudden wanted to be my friends. So it was an odd time. It wasn't what most people perceived. It took years before I could even hold that silver medal. I was ashamed of it.

How much of a blow was it when the U.S. didn't go to the 1980 Olympics? How did you mentally reset for 1984?

I didn't know if I had it in me, because at the time, diving was something I was good at—I was the world champion—but I wasn't particularly enjoying it. It was between '84 and '88 that I realized I really loved the sport.

What made the difference?

Ron, because he knew I was a performer. I was winning competitions, but I wasn't being challenged. So he devised goals for me, like breaking 700 points on the three-meter springboard and the 10-meter platform in the scoring system we had. To achieve that, you couldn't be looking to the side and saying, "I have to beat that person." You had to have the balls to leave everybody behind.

You mentioned being bullied in school. Even after you were an Olympic medalist, your teammates called you names. How did you continue to work and excel in that sort of environment?

It's all in the interpretation. If they called me names, I was flattered by it. I thought, *Obviously they feel threatened by me, and if they can't beat me on the board, they're going to try to unbalance me off it. But we'll see who gets the job done.*

Your teammates knew you were gay, but the viewing public didn't. Why is that?

A lot of people ask me, "When did you come out?" And I say, "It depends on who you ask." I went to the University of Miami, far away from where I grew up, and was in the theater department, so I met other gay people and was out to most of the people there. I came out to my mom in '83. I had a rather volatile breakup with someone and asked her to help me pack my stuff up. We got the van loaded, and I turned to her and said, "Mom, Kevin and I were more than just roommates. We were lovers." And she said, "Oh, I know, son. What's for dinner?" I thought if my parents ever found out I was gay, they wouldn't accept me. But it wasn't that big a deal. So I was out to friends and family. It wasn't a secret. But it was just my policy not to discuss my personal life with members of the media.

After the Olympics, you signed very few endorsement deals. Wheaties didn't put you on the box as part of its Legends series until this year. What did companies tell you or your spokespeople at the time?

I got a few local things but nothing big. A reporter in Chicago contacted Wheaties back in the 1980s to ask why I hadn't been on a box, and the response to him at the time was "We didn't feel that he fulfilled our demographics," which was basically a nice way of saying, "It's rumored that he's gay." That was kind of the mentality. But you never know. In '84 there were so many incredible stories: Edwin Moses, Evelyn Ashford, Carl Lewis, Nancy Hogshead, Rowdy Gaines—all Olympic gold medalists. But the advertising world just totally rallied around Mary Lou Retton. And it was great for her. It's not like we're in competition with each other with this kind of stuff. You just never know who's going to strike a chord.

How do you feel now that you have your Wheaties box?

It's more meaningful now than it would have been in my heyday, because I'm being embraced as a whole person. I'm 56, a gay man, living with HIV, happily married. Who would have imagined that back in the 1980s? I also did some research and found that General Mills is ranked very high in terms of human rights: They have a diversity foundation, and they do a lot for the LGBT community. So the times have changed. We've just come so far.

You retired after the 1988 Games. How did you know that was the right time?

By the time '88 rolled around, the Chinese had caught up to me. They were coming on really strong, and I was holding on by the skin of my teeth. And six months prior to that Olympics, I was diagnosed as HIV-positive, which at that time we thought of as a death sentence. Those were my last competitive dives because I didn't think I would see 30.

Why did you decide to come out publicly as gay and HIV-positive when you did?

I had a scare in '93. We couldn't figure out what was going on. I was losing weight, just wasting away. And so I told my partner and my mom that they could give me a birthday party because I thought I was saying good-bye to everybody. Then I flew out to Florida, checked in to the hospital under an assumed name, got on the right meds. Then I did a play, *Jeffrey*, in New York, and was cast as Darius, who was out and proud. He dies in the play, but his spirit comes back to address the lead character, encouraging him to hate AIDS, not life. There was progress being made. I was around, viable, healthy, and just going about my business, but I also felt very alone and isolated. So I reached out to a friend and said, "I want to write a book." He introduced me to Eric Marcus, who became my coauthor, and we started working. I had friends in the media I could have gone to, but I didn't want to be just a headline. I wanted to explain my story, because there was a lot there. I was going through an abusive relationship and depression. I had tried to commit suicide. So I thought the only way that I could reflect on and share my story was through a book.

You've described yourself as extremely shy, yet you've become something of a spokesperson for LGBT causes. How did you make that transition?

My mom always taught me, "Make everywhere you go better because you were there." It's funny, because I just got an e-mail from my sixth-grade teacher, who asked, "What happened to that shy little 12-year-old that I used to teach?" And you know what? That boy is still here. It's just that I'm more comfortable articulating and sharing my thoughts and feelings now. But it's not a mantle you pick up overnight.

Why are you a mentor and not a coach?

My coach, Ron, was also a mentor. He would meet with us and map out the calendar, saying, "OK, what are the major competitions and what are our goals—diving-related or not?" He coached us as individuals. There is less of that now. So when I meet with athletes, some of it's about diving or communication breakdowns with their coaches, because I don't see the dives the same way they do. They're thinking about the mechanics and the positioning, while I see the athlete holding on to stress and forgetting to breathe. So I'll say, "Put a breath right here and everything else will fall into place." But most of it is about what goes on outside the pool. What are their career aspirations? Where do they see themselves in two to five years? Are they taking action steps to pursue those goals? I take a more holistic approach.

What do you tell mentees about how to manage their post-athletic careers?

Have a plan, but be patient. We are so conditioned to think that our lives revolve around the quadrennial and competitions keep us on track. But you can be on a project for 10 years and then finally see it come to fruition in the 11th.

Originally published in July–August 2016. Reprint R1607L

The Making of a Corporate Athlete

by Jim Loehr and Tony Schwartz

IF THERE IS ONE QUALITY that executives seek for themselves and their employees, it is sustained high performance in the face of ever-increasing pressure and rapid change. But the source of such performance is as elusive as the fountain of youth. Management theorists have long sought to identify precisely what makes some people flourish under pressure and others fold. We maintain that they have come up with only partial answers: rich material rewards, the right culture, management by objectives.

The problem with most approaches, we believe, is that they deal with people only from the neck up, connecting high performance primarily with cognitive capacity. In recent years there has been a growing focus on the relationship between emotional intelligence and high performance. A few theorists have addressed the spiritual dimension—how deeper values and a sense of purpose influence performance. Almost no one has paid any attention to the role played by physical capacities. A successful approach to sustained high performance, we have found, must pull together all of these elements and consider the person as a whole. Thus, our integrated theory of performance management addresses the body, the emotions, the mind, and the spirit. We call this hierarchy the *performance pyramid*. Each of its levels profoundly influences the others, and failure to address any one of them compromises performance.

Our approach has its roots in the two decades that Jim Loehr and his colleagues at LGE spent working with world-class athletes. Several years ago, the two of us began to develop a more comprehensive version of these techniques for executives facing unprecedented demands in the workplace. In effect, we realized, these executives are "corporate athletes." If they were to perform at high levels over the long haul, we posited, they would have to train in the same systematic, multilevel way that world-class athletes do. We have now tested our model on thousands of executives. Their dramatically improved work performance and their enhanced health and happiness confirm our initial hypothesis. In the pages that follow, we describe our approach in detail.

Ideal Performance State

In training athletes, we have never focused on their primary skills—how to hit a serve, swing a golf club, or shoot a basketball. Likewise, in business we don't address primary competencies such as public speaking, negotiating, or analyzing a balance sheet. Our efforts aim instead to help executives build their capacity for what might be called supportive or secondary competencies, among them endurance, strength, flexibility, self-control, and focus. Increasing capacity at all levels allows athletes and executives alike to bring their talents and skills to full ignition and to sustain high performance over time—a condition we call the *Ideal Performance State* (IPS). Obviously, executives can perform successfully even if they smoke, drink and weigh too much, or lack emotional skills or a higher purpose for working. But they cannot perform to their full potential or without a cost over time—to themselves, to their families, and to the corporations for which they work. Put simply, the best long-term performers tap into positive energy at all levels of the performance pyramid.

Extensive research in sports science has confirmed that the capacity to mobilize energy on demand is the foundation of IPS. Our own work has demonstrated that effective energy management has two key components. The first is the rhythmic movement between energy expenditure (stress) and energy renewal (recovery), which we term "oscillation." In the living laboratory of sports, we learned that the real enemy of high performance is not stress, which, para-doxical as it may seem, is actually the stimulus for growth. Rather, the problem is the absence of disciplined, intermittent recovery. Chronic stress without recovery depletes energy reserves, leads to burnout and breakdown, and ultimately undermines performance. Rituals that promote oscillation—rhythmic stress and recovery—are the second component of high performance. Repeated regularly, these highly precise, consciously developed routines become auto-matic over time.

The same methods that enable world-class athletes to reach IPS under pressure, we theorized, would be at least equally effective for business leaders—and perhaps even more important in their lives. The demands on executives to sustain high performance day in and day out, year in and year out, dwarf the challenges faced by any athlete we have ever trained. The average professional athlete, for example, spends most of his time practicing and only a small percentage—several hours a day, at most—actually competing. The typical executive, by contrast, devotes almost no time to training and must perform on demand ten, 12, 14 hours a day or more. Ath-letes enjoy several months of off-season, while most executives are fortunate to get three or four weeks of vacation a year. The career of the average professional athlete spans seven years; the average executive can expect to work 40 to 50 years.

Of course, even corporate athletes who train at all levels will have bad days and run into challenges they can't overcome. Life is tough, and for many time-starved executives, it is only getting tougher. But that is precisely our point. While it isn't always in our power to change our external conditions, we can train to better manage our inner state. We aim to help corporate athletes use the full range of their capaci-ties to thrive in the most difficult circumstances and to emerge from stressful periods stronger, healthier, and eager for the next challenge.

Physical Capacity

Energy can be defined most simply as the capacity to do work. Our training process begins at the physical level because the body is our fundamental source of energy—the foundation of the performance pyramid. Perhaps the best paradigm for building capacity is weight lifting. Several decades of sports science research have established that the key to increasing physical strength is a phenomenon known as supercompensation—essentially the creation of balanced work-rest ratios. In weight lifting, this involves stressing a muscle to the point where its fibers literally start to break down. Given an adequate period of recovery (typically at least 48 hours), the muscle will not only heal, it will grow stronger. But persist in stressing the muscle without rest and the result will be acute and chronic damage. Conversely, failure to stress the muscle results in weakness and atrophy. (Just think of an arm in a cast for several weeks.) In both cases, the enemy is not stress, it's linearity—the failure to oscillate between energy expenditure and recovery.

We first understood the power of rituals to prompt recovery by observing world-class tennis players in the crucible of match play. The best competitors, we discovered, use precise recovery rituals in the 15 or 20 seconds *between* points—often without even being aware of it. Their between-point routines include concentrating on the strings of their rackets to avoid distraction, assuming a confident posture, and visualizing how they want the next point to play out. These routines have startling physiological effects. When we hooked players up to heart rate monitors during their matches, the competitors with the most consistent rituals showed dramatic oscillation, their heart rates rising rapidly during play and then dropping as much as 15% to 20% between points.

The mental and emotional effects of precise between-point routines are equally significant. They allow players to avoid negative feelings, focus their minds, and prepare for the next point. By contrast, players who lack between-point rituals, or who practice them inconsistently, become linear—they expend too much energy without recovery. Regardless of their talent or level of fitness, they become more vulnerable to frustration, anxiety, and loss of concentration and far more likely to choke under pressure.

The same lesson applies to the corporate athletes we train. The problem, we explain, is not so much that their lives are increasingly stressful as that they are so relentlessly linear. Typically, they push themselves too hard mentally and emotionally and too little physically. Both forms of linearity undermine performance.

When we began working with Marilyn Clark, a managing director of Salomon Smith Barney, she had almost no oscillation in her life. Clark, who is in her late 30s, runs the firm's Cleveland office. She is also the mother of three young children, and her husband is a high-powered executive in his own right. To all appearances, Clark lives an enviable life, and she was loath to complain about it. Yet her hectic lifestyle was exacting a cost, which became clear after some probing. In the mornings, temporarily fueled by coffee and a muffin, she was alert and energetic. By the afternoon, though, her energy sagged, and she got through the rest of the day on sheer willpower. At lunchtime, when she could have taken a few quiet moments to recover, she found that she couldn't say no to employees who lined up at her office seeking counsel and support. Between the demands of her job, her colleagues, and her family, she had almost no time for herself. Her frustration quietly grew.

We began our work with Clark by taking stock of her physical capacity. While she had been a passionate athlete as a teenager and an All-American lacrosse player in college, her fitness regimen for the past several years had been limited to occasional sit-ups before bedtime. As she learned more about the relationship between energy and high performance, Clark agreed that her first priority was to get back in shape. She wanted to feel better physically, and she knew from past experience that her mood would improve if she built regular workouts into her schedule.

Because old habits die hard, we helped Clark establish positive rituals to replace them. Part of the work was creating a supportive environment. The colleagues with whom Clark trained became a source of cheerleading—and even nagging—as she established a routine that would have previously seemed unthinkable. Clark committed to work out in a nearby gym three days a week, precisely at 1 p.m. She also enlisted her husband to watch the kids so that she could get in a workout on Saturdays and Sundays.

The High-Performance Pyramid

PEAK PERFORMANCE IN BUSINESS has often been presented as a matter of sheer brainpower, but we view performance as a pyramid. Physical well-being is its foundation. Above that rests emotional health, then mental acuity, and at the top, a sense of purpose. The Ideal Performance State—peak performance under pressure—is achieved when all levels are working together.

Rituals that promote oscillation—the rhythmic expenditure and recovery of energy—link the levels of the pyramid. For instance, vigorous exercise can produce a sense of emotional well-being, clearing the way for peak mental performance.

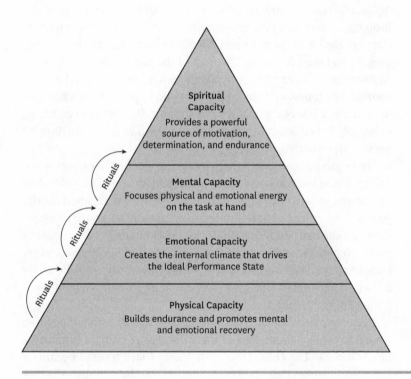

Regular workouts have helped Clark create clear work-life boundaries and restored her sense of herself as an athlete. Now, rather than tumbling into an energy trough in the afternoons and reaching for a candy bar, Clark returns to the office from her workouts feeling reenergized and better able to focus. Physical stress has become a source not just of greater endurance but also of emotional and mental recovery; Clark finds that she can work fewer hours and get more done. And finally, because she no longer feels chronically overburdened, she believes that she has become a better boss. "My body feels reawakened," she says. "I'm much more relaxed, and the resentment I was feeling about all the demands on me is gone."

Clark has inspired other members of her firm to take out health club memberships. She and several colleagues are subsidizing employees who can't easily afford the cost. "We're not just talking to each other about business accolades and who is covering which account," she says. "Now it's also about whether we got our workouts in and how well we're recovering. We're sharing something healthy, and that has brought people together."

The corporate athlete doesn't build a strong physical foundation by exercise alone, of course. Good sleeping and eating rituals are integral to effective energy management. When we first met Rudy Borneo, the vice chairman of Macy's West, he complained of erratic energy levels, wide mood swings, and difficulty concentrating. He was also overweight. Like many executives—and most Americans—his eating habits were poor. He typically began his long, travel-crammed days by skipping breakfast—the equivalent of rolling to the start line of the Indianapolis 500 with a near-empty fuel tank. Lunch was catch-as-catch-can, and Borneo used sugary snacks to fight off his inevitable afternoon hunger pangs. These foods spiked his blood glucose levels, giving him a quick jolt of energy, but one that faded quickly. Dinner was often a rich, multicourse meal eaten late in the evening. Digesting that much food disturbed Borneo's sleep and left him feeling sluggish and out of sorts in the mornings.

Sound familiar?

As we did with Clark, we helped Borneo replace his bad habits with positive rituals, beginning with the way he ate. We explained that by eating lightly but often, he could sustain a steady level of energy. (For a fuller account of the foundational exercise, eating, and sleep routines, see the sidebar "A Firm Foundation.") Borneo now eats breakfast every day—typically a high-protein drink rather than coffee and a bagel. We also showed him research by chronobiologists suggesting that the body and mind need recovery every 90 to 120 minutes. Using that cycle as the basis for his eating schedule, he installed a refrigerator by his desk and began eating five or six small but nutritious meals a day and sipping water frequently. He also shifted the emphasis in his workouts to interval training, which increased his endurance and speed of recovery.

In addition to prompting weight loss and making him feel better, Borneo's nutritional and fitness rituals have had a dramatic effect on other aspects of his life. "I now exercise for my mind as much as for my body," he says. "At the age of 59, I have more energy than ever, and I can sustain it for a longer period of time. For me, the rituals are the holy grail. Using them to create balance has had an impact on every aspect of my life: staying more positive, handling difficult human resource issues, dealing with change, treating people better. I really do believe that when you learn to take care of yourself, you free up energy and enthusiasm to care more for others."

Emotional Capacity

The next building block of IPS is emotional capacity—the internal climate that supports peak performance. During our early research, we asked hundreds of athletes to describe how they felt when they were performing at their best. Invariably, they used words such as "calm," "challenged," "engaged," "focused," "optimistic," and "confident." As sprinter Marion Jones put it shortly after winning one of her gold medals at the Olympic Games in Sydney: "I'm out here having a ball. This is not a stressful time in my life. This is a very happy time." When we later asked the same question of law enforcement officers, military personnel, surgeons, and corporate executives, they used remarkably similar language to describe their Ideal Performance State.

Just as positive emotions ignite the energy that drives high performance, negative emotions—frustration, impatience, anger, fear, resentment, and sadness—drain energy. Over time, these feelings can be literally toxic, elevating heart rate and blood pressure, increasing muscle tension, constricting vision, and ultimately crippling performance. Anxious, fear ridden athletes are far more likely to choke in competition, for example, while anger and frustration sabotage their capacity for calm focus.

The impact of negative emotions on business performance is subtler but no less devastating. Alan, an executive at an investment company, travels frequently, overseeing a half-dozen offices around the country. His colleagues and subordinates, we learned, considered him to be a perfectionist and an often critical boss whose frustration and impatience sometimes boiled over into angry tirades. Our work focused on helping Alan find ways to manage his emotions more effectively. His anger, we explained, was a reactive emotion, a fight-or-flight response to situations he perceived as threatening. To manage more effectively, he needed to transform his inner experience of threat under stress into one of challenge.

A regular workout regimen built Alan's endurance and gave him a way to burn off tension. But because his fierce travel schedule often got in the way of his workouts, we also helped him develop a precise five-step ritual to contain his negative emotions whenever they threatened to erupt. His initial challenge was to become more aware of signals from his body that he was on edge—physical tension, a racing heart, tightness in his chest. When he felt those sensations arise, his first step was to close his eyes and take several deep breaths. Next, he consciously relaxed the muscles in his face. Then, he made an effort to soften his voice and speak more slowly. After that, he tried to put himself in the shoes of the person who was the target of his anger—to imagine what he or she must be feeling. Finally, he focused on framing his response in positive language.

Instituting this ritual felt awkward to Alan at first, not unlike trying to learn a new golf swing. More than once he reverted to his old behavior. But within several weeks, the five-step drill had become automatic—a highly reliable way to short-circuit his reactivity.

A Firm Foundation

HERE ARE OUR BASIC STRATEGIES FOR renewing energy at the physical level. Some of them are so familiar they've become background noise, easy to ignore. That's why we're repeating them. If any of these strategies aren't part of your life now, their absence may help account for fatigue, irritability, lack of emotional resilience, difficulty concentrating, and even a flagging sense of purpose.

1. Actually do all those healthy things you know you ought to do

Eat five or six small meals a day; people who eat just one or two meals a day with long periods in between force their bodies into a conservation mode, which translates into slower metabolism. Always eat breakfast: eating first thing in the morning sends your body the signal that it need not slow metabolism to conserve energy. Eat a balanced diet. Despite all the conflicting nutritional research, over-whelming evidence suggests that a healthy dietary ratio is 50% to 60% complex carbohydrates, 25% to 35% protein, and 20% to 25% fat. Dramatically reduce simple sugars. In addition to representing empty calories, sugar causes energy-depleting spikes in blood glucose levels. Drink four to five 12-ounce glasses of water daily, even if you don't feel thirsty. As much as half the population walks around with mild chronic dehydration. And finally, on the "you know you should" list: get physically active. We strongly recommend three to four 20- to 30-minute cardiovascular workouts a week, including at least two sessions of intervals—short bursts of intense exertion followed by brief recovery periods.

2. Go to bed early and wake up early

Night owls have a much more difficult time dealing with the demands of to-day's business world, because typically, they still have to get up with the early

Numerous employees reported that he had become more reasonable, more approachable, and less scary. Alan himself says that he has become a far more effective manager.

Through our work with athletes, we have learned a number of other rituals that help to offset feelings of stress and restore positive energy. It's no coincidence, for example, that many athletes wear headphones as they prepare for competition. Music has powerful physiological and emotional effects. It can prompt a shift in mental activity from the rational left hemisphere of the brain to the more intuitive right hemisphere. It also provides a relief from obsessive thinking and worrying. Finally, music can be a means of directly birds. They're often groggy and unfocused in the mornings, dependent on caffeine and sugary snacks to keep up their energy. You can establish new sleep rituals. Biological clocks are not fixed in our genes.

3. Maintain a consistent bedtime and wake-up time

As important as the number of hours you sleep (ideally seven to eight) is the consistency of the recovery wave you create. Regular sleep cycles help regulate your other biological clocks and increase the likelihood that the sleep you get will be deep and restful.

4. Seek recovery every 90 to 120 minutes

Chronobiologists have found that the body's hormone, glucose, and blood pressure levels drop every 90 minutes or so. By failing to seek recovery and overriding the body's natural stress-rest cycles, overall capacity is compromised. As we've learned from athletes, even short, focused breaks can promote significant recovery. We suggest five sources of restoration: eat something, hydrate, move physically, change channels mentally, and change channels emotionally.

5. Do at least two weight-training workouts a week

No form of exercise more powerfully turns back the markers of age than weight training. It increases strength, retards osteoporosis, speeds up metabolism, enhances mobility, improves posture, and dramatically increases energy.

regulating energy—raising it when the time comes to perform and lowering it when it is more appropriate to decompress.

Body language also influences emotions. In one well-known experiment, actors were asked to portray anger and then were subjected to numerous physiological tests, including heart rate, blood pressure, core temperature, galvanic skin response, and hormone levels. Next, the actors were exposed to a situation that made them genuinely angry, and the same measurements were taken. There were virtually no differences in the two profiles. Effective acting produces precisely the same physiology that real emotions do. All great athletes understand this instinctively. If they carry themselves confidently, they will eventually start to feel confident, even in highly stressful situations. That's why we train our corporate clients to "act as if"—consciously creating the look on the outside that they want to feel on the inside. "You are what you repeatedly do," said Aristotle. "Excellence is not a singular act but a habit."

Close relationships are perhaps the most powerful means for prompting positive emotions and effective recovery. Anyone who has enjoyed a happy family reunion or an evening with good friends knows the profound sense of safety and security that these relationships can induce. Such feelings are closely associated with the Ideal Performance State. Unfortunately, many of the corporate athletes we train believe that in order to perform up to expectations at work, they have no choice but to stint on their time with loved ones. We try to reframe the issue. By devoting more time to their most important relationships and setting clearer boundaries between work and home, we tell our clients, they will not only derive more satisfaction but will also get the recovery that they need to perform better at work.

Mental Capacity

The third level of the performance pyramid—the cognitive—is where most traditional performance-enhancement training is aimed. The usual approaches tend to focus on improving competencies by using techniques such as process reengineering and knowledge management or by learning to use more sophisticated technology. Our training aims to enhance our clients' cognitive capacities—most notably their focus, time management, and positive- and critical-thinking skills.

Focus simply means energy concentrated in the service of a particular goal. Anything that interferes with focus dissipates energy. Meditation, typically viewed as a spiritual practice, can serve as a highly practical means of training attention and promoting recovery. At this level, no guidance from a guru is required. A perfectly adequate meditation technique involves sitting quietly and breathing deeply, counting each exhalation, and starting over when you reach ten. Alternatively, you can choose a word to repeat each time you take a breath.

Practiced regularly, meditation quiets the mind, the emotions, and the body, promoting energy recovery. Numerous studies have shown, for example, that experienced meditators need considerably fewer hours of sleep than nonmeditators. Meditation and other non-cognitive disciplines can also slow brain wave activity and stimulate a shift in mental activity from the left hemisphere of the brain to the right. Have you ever suddenly found the solution to a vexing problem while doing something "mindless" such as jogging, working in the garden, or singing in the shower? That's the left-brain, right-brain shift at work—the fruit of mental oscillation.

Much of our training at this level focuses on helping corporate athletes to consciously manage their time and energy. By alternating periods of stress with renewal, they learn to align their work with the body's need for breaks every 90 to 120 minutes. This can be challenging for compulsive corporate achievers. Jeffrey Sklar, 39, managing director for institutional sales at the New York investment firm Gruntal & Company, had long been accustomed to topping his competitors by brute force—pushing harder and more relentlessly than anyone else. With our help, he built a set of rituals that ensured regular recovery and also enabled him to perform at a higher level while spending fewer hours at work.

Once in the morning and again in the afternoon, Sklar retreats from the frenetic trading floor to a quiet office, where he spends 15 minutes doing deep-breathing exercises. At lunch, he leaves the office—something he once would have found unthinkable—and walks outdoors for at least 15 minutes. He also works out five or six times a week after work. At home, he and his wife, Sherry, a busy executive herself, made a pact never to talk business after 8 p.m. They also swore off work on the weekends, and they have stuck to their vow for nearly two years. During each of those years, Sklar's earnings have increased by more than 65%.

For Jim Connor, the president and CEO of FootJoy, reprioritizing his time became a way not just to manage his energy better but to create more balance in his life and to revive his sense of passion. Connor had come to us saying that he felt stuck in a deep rut. "My feelings were muted so I could deal with the emotional pain of life," he explains. "I had smoothed out all the vicissitudes in my life to such an extent that oscillation was prohibited. I was not feeling life but repetitively performing it."

Connor had imposed on himself the stricture that he be the first person to arrive at the office each day and the last to leave. In reality, he acknowledged, no one would object if he arrived a little later or left a little earlier a couple of days a week. He realized it also made sense for him to spend one or two days a week working at a satellite plant 45 minutes nearer to his home than his main office. Doing so could boost morale at the second plant while cutting 90 minutes from his commute.

Immediately after working with us, Connor arranged to have an office cleared out at the satellite factory. He now spends at least one full day a week there, prompting a number of people at that office to comment to him about his increased availability. He began taking a golf lesson one morning a week, which also allowed for a more relaxed drive to his main office, since he commutes there after rush hour on golf days. In addition, he instituted a monthly getaway routine with his wife. In the evenings, he often leaves his office earlier in order to spend more time with his family.

Connor has also meticulously built recovery into his workdays. "What a difference these fruit and water breaks make," he says. "I set my alarm watch for 90 minutes to prevent relapses, but I'm instinctively incorporating this routine into my life and love it. I'm far more productive as a result, and the quality of my thought process is measurably improved. I'm also doing more on the big things at work and not getting bogged down in detail. I'm pausing more to think and to take time out."

Rituals that encourage positive thinking also increase the likelihood of accessing the Ideal Performance State. Once again, our work with top athletes has taught us the power of creating specific mental rituals to sustain positive energy. Jack Nicklaus, one of the greatest pressure performers in the history of golf, seems to have an intuitive understanding of the importance of both oscillation and rituals. "I've developed a regimen that allows me to move from peaks of concentration into valleys of relaxation and back again as necessary," he wrote in *Golf Digest*. "My focus begins to sharpen as I walk onto the tee and steadily intensifies . . . until I hit [my drive]. . . . I descend into a valley as I leave the tee, either through casual conversation with a fellow competitor or by letting my mind dwell on whatever happens into it."

Visualization is another ritual that produces positive energy and has palpable performance results. For example, Earl Woods taught his son Tiger—Nicklaus's heir apparent—to form a mental image of the ball rolling into the hole before each shot. The exercise does more than produce a vague feeling of optimism and well-being. Neuroscientist Ian Robertson of Trinity College, Dublin, author of *Mind Sculpture*, has found that visualization can literally reprogram the neural circuitry of the brain, directly improving performance. It is hard to imagine a better illustration than diver Laura Wilkinson. Six months before the summer Olympics in Sydney, Wilkinson broke three toes on her right foot while training. Unable to go in the water because of her cast, she instead spent hours a day on the diving platform, visualizing each of her dives. With only a few weeks to actually practice before the Olympics, she pulled off a huge upset, winning the gold medal on the ten-meter platform.

Visualization works just as well in the office. Sherry Sklar has a ritual to prepare for any significant event in her work life. "I always take time to sit down in advance in a quiet place and think about what I really want from the meeting," she says. "Then I visualize myself achieving the outcome I'm after." In effect, Sklar is building mental muscles—increasing her strength, endurance, and flexibility. By doing so, she decreases the likelihood that she will be distracted by negative thoughts under pressure. "It has made me much more relaxed and confident when I go into presentations," she says.

Spiritual Capacity

Most executives are wary of addressing the spiritual level of the performance pyramid in business settings, and understandably so. The word "spiritual" prompts conflicting emotions and doesn't seem immediately relevant to high performance. So let's be clear: by spiritual capacity, we simply mean the energy that is unleashed by tapping into one's deepest values and defining a strong sense of purpose. This capacity, we have found, serves as sustenance in the face of adversity and as a powerful source of motivation, focus, determination, and resilience.

Consider the case of Ann, a high-level executive at a large cosmetics company. For much of her adult life, she has tried unsuccessfully to quit smoking, blaming her failures on a lack of self-discipline. Smoking took a visible toll on her health and her productivity at work—decreased endurance from shortness of breath, more sick days than her colleagues, and nicotine cravings that distracted her during long meetings.

Four years ago, when Ann became pregnant, she was able to quit immediately and didn't touch a cigarette until the day her child was born, when she began smoking again. A year later, Ann became pregnant for a second time, and again she stopped smoking, with virtually no symptoms of withdrawal. True to her pattern, she resumed smoking when her child was born. "I don't understand it," she told us plaintively.

We offered a simple explanation. As long as Ann was able to connect the impact of smoking to a deeper purpose—the health of her unborn child—quitting was easy. She was able to make what we call a "values-based adaptation." But without a strong connection to a deeper sense of purpose, she went back to smoking—an expedient adaptation that served her short-term interests. Smoking was a sensory pleasure for Ann, as well as a way to allay her anxiety and manage social stress. Understanding cognitively that it was unhealthy, feeling guilty about it on an emotional level, and even experiencing its negative effects physically were all insufficient motivations to change her behavior. To succeed, Ann needed a more sustaining source of motivation.

Making such a connection, we have found, requires regularly stepping off the endless treadmill of deadlines and obligations to take time for reflection. The inclination for busy executives is to live in a perpetual state of triage, doing whatever seems most immediately pressing while losing sight of any bigger picture. Rituals that give people the opportunity to pause and look inside include meditation, journal writing, prayer, and service to others. Each of these activities can also serve as a source of recovery—a way to break the linearity of relentless goal-oriented activity.

Taking the time to connect to one's deepest values can be extremely rewarding. It can also be painful, as a client we'll call Richard discovered. Richard is a stockbroker who works in New York City and lives in a distant suburb, where his wife stays at home with their three young children. Between his long commute and his long hours, Richard spent little time with his family. Like so many of our clients, he typically left home before his children woke up and returned around 7:30 in the evening, feeling exhausted and in no mood to talk to anyone. He wasn't happy with his situation, but he saw no easy solution. In time, his unhappiness began to affect his work, which made him even more negative when he got home at night. It was a vicious cycle.

One evening while driving home from work, Richard found himself brooding about his life. Suddenly, he felt so overcome by emotion that he stopped his car at a park ten blocks from home to collect himself. To his astonishment, he began to weep. He felt consumed with grief about his life and filled with longing for his family. After ten minutes, all Richard wanted to do was get home and hug his wife and children. Accustomed to giving their dad a wide berth at the end of the day, his kids were understandably bewildered when he walked in that evening with tears streaming down his face and wrapped them all in hugs. When his wife arrived on the scene, her first thought was that he'd been fired.

The next day, Richard again felt oddly compelled to stop at the park near his house. Sure enough, the tears returned and so did the longing. Once again, he rushed home to his family. During the subsequent two years, Richard was able to count on one hand the number of times that he failed to stop at the same location for at least ten minutes. The rush of emotion subsided over time, but his sense that he was affirming what mattered most in his life remained as strong as ever.

Richard had stumbled into a ritual that allowed him both to disengage from work and to tap into a profound source of purpose and meaning—his family. In that context, going home ceased to be a burden after a long day and became instead a source of recovery and renewal. In turn, Richard's distraction at work diminished, and he became more focused, positive, and productive—so much so that he was able to cut down on his hours. On a practical level, he created a better balance between stress and recovery. Finally, by tapping into a deeper sense of purpose, he found a powerful new source of energy for both his work and his family.

In a corporate environment that is changing at warp speed, performing consistently at high levels is more difficult and more necessary than ever. Narrow interventions simply aren't sufficient anymore. Companies can't afford to address their employees' cognitive capacities while ignoring their physical, emotional, and spiritual well-being. On the playing field or in the boardroom, high performance depends as much on how people renew and recover energy as on how they expend it, on how they manage their lives as much as on how they manage their work. When people feel strong and resilient—physically, mentally, emotionally, and spiritually—they perform better, with more passion, for longer. They win, their families win, and the corporations that employ them win.

Originally published in January 2001. Reprint R0101H

The Tough Work of Turning Around a Team

by Bill Parcells

THE PEOPLE IN YOUR COMPANY have little loyalty; some even want you to fail. Your star performers expect constant pampering. Your stockholders are impatient, demanding quick results. And the media scrutinize and second-guess your every move.

I can relate.

As a coach in the NFL, I've been in a lot of pressure-cooker situations, and my guess is that the challenges I've faced are not all that different from the ones that executives deal with every day. I'm not saying that business is like football. I am saying that people are people, and that the keys to motivating them and getting them to perform to their full potential are pretty much the same whether they're playing on a football field or working in an office.

The toughest challenge I've faced as a coach is taking a team that's performing poorly and turning it around. I've done it three times now. In 1983, my first year as a head coach, I led the New York Giants through an abysmal season—we won only three games. In the next six seasons, we climbed to the top of the league, winning two Super Bowls. When I became coach of the New England Patriots in 1993, they were coming off two years in which they'd won a combined total of three games. In 1996, we were in the Super Bowl. In 1997, when I came to the New York Jets, the team had just suffered through a 1-15 season. Two years later, we made it to the conference championship.

Those turnarounds taught me a fundamental lesson about leadership: You have to be honest with people—brutally honest. You have to tell them the truth about their performance, you have to tell it to them face-to-face, and you have to tell it to them over and over again. Sometimes the truth will be painful, and sometimes saying it will lead to an uncomfortable confrontation. So be it. The only way to change people is to tell them in the clearest possible terms what they're doing wrong. And if they don't want to listen, they don't belong on the team.

Taking Charge

To lead, you've got to be a leader. That may sound obvious, but it took me an entire year to learn—and it wasn't a pleasant year. When I started as coach of the Giants, I lacked confidence. I was surrounded by star players with big names and big egos, and I was a little tentative in dealing with them. I didn't confront them about how they needed to change to succeed. As a result, I didn't get their respect and I wasn't able to change their attitudes. So they just kept on with their habit of losing.

At the end of the season, I figured I'd be fired. But management ended up asking me back for another season—mainly because they couldn't find anybody to replace me. At that point, I knew I had nothing to lose, so I decided I would do it my way. I was going to lead and the players were going to follow, and that's all there was to it. On the first day of training camp, I laid it on the line: I told everyone that losing would no longer be tolerated. Players who were contributing to the team's weak performance would be given a chance to change, and if they didn't change, they'd be gone.

It was a tough message, but I balanced it with a more positive one. I told them what I think a team is all about: achievement. Sure, they could make a lot of money in football and they could buy a lot of nice things, but the only permanent value of work lies in achievement, and that comes only with relentless effort and commitment. It wasn't going to be easy, but at the end of the day, achievement would be the most important thing they would take home with them.

After I talked to them as a group and established my credibility as a leader, I began talking with them personally. With the Giants, and with the other teams I've coached, I've found that holding frank, one-on-one conversations with every member of the organization is essential to success. It allows me to ask each player for his support in helping the team achieve its goals, and it allows me to explain exactly what I expect from him. I try to appeal to the players' passion for achievement and winning, but I'm also very clear that if they don't give the team what it needs, then I'm going to find someone else who will. I tell them, "If you don't want to play in the championship games and you don't want to achieve at the highest level, then I don't want you here, because that's what I'm trying to do. I am not trying to finish fourth." Leaders can do everything right with their teams and still fail if they don't deliver their message to each member as an individual.

Those conversations also give me a basis for making an honest evaluation of every player. It's all too easy to come into an organization that's been struggling and make blanket judgments about everybody–to think everybody's failing. But that's a mistake. There can be many hidden strengths on a team, just as there can be many hidden weaknesses. The only way you can bring them to the surface is by watching and talking with each team member. You'll quickly see who's a contributor and who's an obstacle. And, for the good of the team, you'll want to move swiftly to get the obstacles out of the way. The hard fact is that some people will never change.

So if you're called in to turn around a team, here's Rule One: make it clear from day one that you're in charge. Don't wait to earn your leadership; impose it.

The Power of Confrontation

If you want to get the most out of people, you have to apply pressure—that's the only thing that any of us really responds to. As a coach, I've always tried to turn up the heat under my people, to constantly push them to perform at a high level.

Creating pressure in an organization requires confrontation, and it can get very intense, very emotional. I've seen coaches avoid confrontations with their players because they don't like conflict, and I assume the same thing is true among the leaders of business teams.

But I've actually come to relish confrontation, not because it makes me feel powerful but because it provides an opportunity to get things straight with people. It's not until you look people right in the eye that you get to the sources of their behavior and motivation. Without confrontation, you're not going to change the way they think and act.

Confrontation does not mean putting someone down. When you criticize members of the team, you need to put it in a positive context. I've often said to a player, "I don't think you're performing up to your potential; you can do better." But I also made it clear that my goals were his goals: "It's in your best interest that you succeed, and it's in my best interest that you succeed. We really want the same thing." Once you set that context, though, you shouldn't be afraid to be blunt about people's failings. You shouldn't be afraid to offend them. You need to do what it takes to get a strong reaction because then you know you've reached them.

In the end, I've found, people like the direct approach. It's much more valuable to them to have a leader who's absolutely clear and open than to have one who soft-soaps or talks in circles. I've had many players come back to me ten years later and thank me for putting the pressure on them. They say what they remember most about me is one line: "I think you're better than you think you are." In fact, they say they use the same line with their kids when they're not doing so well in school or are having other problems. My father used that expression with me, and there's a lot of truth to it—people can do more than they think they can.

That's Rule Two: confrontation is healthy.

Success Breeds Success

The prospect of going from a team that's at the bottom of the standings to one that's on top is daunting. When you've done a lot of losing, it gets hard to imagine yourself winning. So even as I'm confronting players about their weaknesses, I'm also always trying to build a culture of success. That's not something you can do overnight. You have to go one step at a time, the same way you move the ball down the field, yard by yard.

Here's my philosophy: to win games, you need to believe as a team that you have the ability to win games. That is, confidence is born only of demonstrated ability. This may sound like a catch-22, but it's important to remember that even small successes can be extremely powerful in helping people believe in themselves.

In training camp, therefore, we don't focus on the ultimate goal—getting to the Super Bowl. We establish a clear set of goals that are within immediate reach: we're going to be a smart team; we're going to be a well-conditioned team; we're going to be a team that plays hard; we're going to be a team that has pride; we're going to be a team that wants to win collectively; we're going to be a team that doesn't criticize one another.

When we start acting in ways that fulfill these goals, I make sure everybody knows it. I accentuate the positive at every possible opportunity, and at the same time I emphasize the next goal that we need to fulfill. If we have a particularly good practice, then I call the team together and say, "We got something done today; we executed real well. I'm very pleased with your work. But here's what I want to do tomorrow: I want to see flawless special teams work. If you accomplish that, then we'll be ready for the game on Sunday."

When you set small, visible goals, and people achieve them, they start to get it into their heads that they can succeed. They break the habit of losing and begin to get into the habit of winning. It's extremely satisfying to see that kind of shift take place in the way a team thinks about itself.

So Rule Three is: set small goals and hit them.

Picking the Right People

Another challenge in building a winning team comes from free agency. I know that companies today are having trouble hanging on to their best people; there's a great deal of turnover and not much loyalty. That's a situation that I had to adapt to as a coach.

One of the things that initially helped me become successful in the NFL was my ability to develop players with the Giants. We had a program in place, and we brought people along slowly. Today, you no longer have the time to develop your talent in the old way. The situation is more like coaching high school football in some respects—every year, the senior class graduates and moves on. When I started, coaches reworked maybe 8% or 10% of their teams every year. Now it's sometimes as high as 30%.

That kind of turnover adds a tough new wrinkle to turning a team around and keeping it on the winning track. In particular, you have to be extremely careful about the new people you bring on. You can do serious damage with a few bad choices. Unfortunately, there's no science to picking the right people. There's a lot of trial and error involved. You're going to get fooled by people, and you're going to make mistakes—I know I've made my share. But after a while, you start to develop a sense of who's likely to work out. I've found it's not always the one who has the best reputation or even the most outstanding set of talents. It's usually the one who understands what it will take to succeed and is committed to making the effort.

For example, there's a player, Bryan Cox, who had a terrible reputation in the NFL. He'd been fined a lot of money by the league—maybe more than anyone in its history. My teams had played against him so many times that I almost felt like I knew him. And watching him play, I'd say to myself, this guy plays so hard and tries so hard—he's got something that I want to have on my team. So when he was a free agent, I called him on the phone and we had a straight, tough talk. I told him exactly what I wanted from him, and he told me what he wanted from me, which boiled down to this: "Don't BS me." I told him he'd always know what I was thinking. Bryan signed on with the Jets, and he's done a great job for the franchise.

I'm no psychologist. I don't care about what kind of personality someone has or whether it corresponds with my own. I don't care if they're "well adjusted." I just want my players to want to win as much as I want to win. I'm convinced that if you get people onto your team who share the same goals and the same passion, and if you push them to achieve at the highest level, you're going to come out on top.

Originally published in November–December 2000. Reprint R00613

An Interview with Alex Gregory

Alex Gregory *is an Olympic rower, World Champion, and father of two. In 2012, he won gold in the coxless four at the London Olympics with teammates Tom James, Andrew Triggs Hodge, and Pete Reed. But success didn't come easy; earlier in his career, he battled nerves and asthma, even blacking out in the water (twice). HBR talked to him about how he learned to thrive under pressure. This is an edited conversation.*
Interviewed by Sarah Green Carmichael

HBR: *You've been really open about how early in your career, you weren't the best at performing under pressure. What would happen?*

Gregory: Although I liked the training, I never really loved the racing. Even at a young age I'd get nervous. In the early days, we were in a crew with two or three other people, and being in a boat with other people helped to calm my nerves. But to really pursue rowing, I had to learn to do it on my own in single scull. And that's when I came into my difficult years, where things would go wrong. Basically it all boiled down to worrying too much about the result. It's wanting something so much and worrying about it so much that you make it not happen. It became a vicious cycle: I'd fail, put even more pressure on myself, panic that I was going to fail, and fail again at the next event.

So how did you start to get your nerves under control?

About eight or nine years after I started rowing, I'd decided I was going to give up. I'd been very lucky to be invited as a spare man for the team going to the 2008 Olympics in Beijing, but I'd decided I wasn't cut out for it and this would be my last event.

But then I got to Beijing. The Olympics is totally different. It's everything. It's what anyone aspires to be at. And sitting there on the sidelines, I just felt like there was something missing. I hadn't achieved what I wanted to achieve.

And I realized that my answer had always been to practice technique. I had very good technique already—that was what had gotten me to where I was. But it was my physical strength that wasn't good enough.

It was like a light switch went on. It was so simple, I couldn't believe I hadn't thought of it before.

I decided to give rowing one last chance. I spent three months just doing weights before I started training again with the guys. I could immediately see results—I was suddenly beating people who had always beaten me. It gave me so much confidence, and that confidence was all I needed.

It's interesting to me that the lynchpin was focusing on improving a weakness. At HBR, we often tell people to focus on their strengths.

It's so easy and much more fun to work on your strengths. You get immediate positive feedback—*you looked great out there, that's perfect, well done!* But the thing you're practicing, well, you were already good at it. You end up improving on that stuff naturally. So I think what you really need to work on is what you're not good at. And I think that's as true in business as it is in sport.

Rowing is unlike any other sport I can think of in the degree to which it balances the tension between competing as individuals and competing as a team. You compete against each other to win a seat in the boat, but then have to really come together as one for the race. How do you do that?

One of the most difficult things is racing against my mates. Andy [Triggs Hodge] and Pete [Reed] are my friends, but we're also competitors. I train every day, seven days a week, 350 days a year with the same 25 guys. Same lake, same day, same time. And for nine months of the year, we are competing against each other to make the seats. As soon as we're brought into a crew by the coaches, we're not competitors, but teammates.

Rowing is all about moving together. Not just a visual thing or an audible thing—it's about feeling it. If someone is even slightly out of sync, that will affect the boat speed. Molding it together comes from the coach watching from the outside, but also from all of us on the boat giving each other feedback.

For example, in 2011 we got in the boat and immediately it worked. We just clicked from the first stroke. It was magical—and we ended up winning the world championship. But when a new crew was selected for the Olympics, we took our first strokes together and it was almost the exact opposite. We were all moving in the right way pretty much, but the magic just wasn't there. There was nothing the coach could see from the outside, and that kind of gets a little bit worrying when you're supposed to be the top four guys in the country and you're expected—and expecting—to win gold.

How did you figure out how to bring the team together then? Because you did end up winning the gold.

We really struggled for the first couple of months. We weren't slow, but we knew that there was something missing. Australia had beaten us in the last [important race] before the Olympics. We knew we had to change something major, but we just couldn't do it. And you can't push back the Olympics if you're not ready. You have to perform on that day. If you don't, you fail.

But we're fortunate in Great Britain to have a great resource in previous rowing champions who are available to talk with. Two of us, Tom [James] and I, went to talk with Matthew Pinsent. He gave us a lot of advice, but basically it boiled down to being totally honest in the boat.

When we got to our next training camp, we all chatted for two hours about what we wanted, what we were trying to achieve. We got down to how we wanted the stroke to look, the technical aspects of it. I could say very openly to Pete, "OK Pete, you need to do this part better." And he could say to me, "Yes, and you're not so good at this bit, Alex." Earlier, I might have taken that personally and not really wanted to do it, because he'd told me to do it [laughs], you know what I mean?

Now the feeling in our boat was different. Earlier, we hadn't been talking about the right things. We had to really take criticism and give criticism in a constructive way. Then for the next seven weeks, we knew exactly what we would be working on, on every stroke for hundreds of thousands of strokes.

So you come back from training camp for the Olympics, and this time, you're not a "spare man." You're on the team. The games are in your home country. And the British team is competing for its fourth consecutive gold medal in this event. To me that sounds like an enormous amount of pressure. How did you deal with it?

The Olympics is unlike any other event—the crowd, the expectations, everything is bigger. There's a buzz. I can't remember the exact statistic, but the number of people who get a gold [medal] at their first Olympics is much smaller compared with people who have been to one before.

So for me, being in this particular crew was great, because the other three guys had won in Beijing. They'd already done it, so I had confidence in them. I can take the pressure off myself when I share that pressure with someone else.

We had also had quite a few discussions about what the pressures would be—of what it would be like to fly back to London having been in the private bubble of working in our own little boats. We were prepared because we'd talked about it beforehand.

Thinking back to earlier in your career, what do you wish you had known about performing under pressure?

That I have to have people around me, first of all. Back when I was racing solo, I'd be in the water on my own, at training camps on my own, in a room on my own. My coach was the only person I'd talk to for six or seven weeks at a time. It was incredibly isolating.

And second, that it always helps to talk about the problems. In those days, I would physically shake on the starting line at the start of a race because I was so scared I'd lose. It was a terrible time for me. But if I had spoken to my coach and been honest with him, then I'm sure he could have helped. It sounds a bit silly, but I was too scared of him thinking I was weak or that I couldn't do it, that he would think I wasn't good enough.

I think that people in all walks of life probably feel that—that they should do it all on their own. Now I think that doing it on your own doesn't mean you can't talk to people, get their advice, and be honest about the problems. You're still the one going out there and doing it.

Originally published in February 2014. Reprint H0008s

Mental Preparation Secrets of Top Athletes, Entertainers, and Surgeons

An interview with Daniel McGinn

by Sarah Green Carmichael

SARAH GREEN CARMICHAEL: *Welcome to the HBR IdeaCast from* Harvard Business Review. *I'm Sarah Green Carmichael. To get psyched up for the big game, sports teammates give each other pep talks, listen to an exciting song during warm-ups, or follow a particular pregame routine. Then there's a locker room speech, often dramatized in popular movies, where the coach inspires individuals to greatness.*

[Excerpt from *Miracle*]:
Herb Brooks: I'm sick and tired of hearing about what a great hockey team the Soviets have. Screw them. This is your time. Now go out there and take it.

But what's the business equivalent of the pep talk? When you have a big presentation, job interview, quarter-ending sales meeting, or situation where you really need to be on, how do you prepare for it? If you're like a lot of people, you probably think about what you're going to say and what you're going to wear, and then you just kind of, well, show up.

HBR's senior editor Dan McGinn thinks we can all do better than that by taking a cue from how the best athletes and performers prepare. He's the author of the article "The Science of Pep Talks" in the July–August 2017 issue of Harvard Business Review, *and he is also the author of the book* Psyched Up: How the Science of Mental Preparation Can Help You Succeed. *Dan, thank you for joining us today.*

Daniel McGinn: Thank you, Sarah.

So did you have to get psyched up to write this book?

I did actually. Writing this book did change the way I get ready to perform my job as a writer every morning or many mornings. If you watch sports, you become pretty accustomed to seeing the athletes and what they do when they warm up. They tend to have headphones on, and you know that they're listening to a certain set of songs. It's not just up to chance. You're used to seeing locker room speeches. You're used to seeing that gaze, that locked-in look that they have, and that focus.

And they're taught to do that. There are sports psychologists who teach them exactly what they should be thinking about before a game. The argument I have is that more of our jobs are like that these days. It's less like factory work where you're doing the same thing every day and more about the big pitch, the presentation, the sales call, and that we should learn to do what these athletes do to try to lock ourselves in.

I think about coming into my job every day and that maybe we should run through the halls and give every editor a high five and then chew a pen and then put the pen back in the bin or other crazy things. How feasible is it to do some of these things on a daily basis?

Yeah, obviously if our boss Adi Ignatius gave us a speech like Knute Rockne did before we sat down to edit articles, we would all think it was kind of crazy. If you don't know who that is, Rockne was the legendary Notre Dame football coach from the 1920s.

So why do people have rituals? And why is there a lot of research that suggests that they work? Well, one theory is that they help us remember how much practice we've done. They help get our bodies and our minds into the groove. The other is that they give us something to focus on other than being nervous and anxious. Think of a funeral. Funerals are very awkward occasions, and there's this whole set of rituals about what we do when we go through it. That's because it's awkward, and we want something to do to not think about the nervousness.

So there's a distractive element to rituals. They just help your body get into the groove. I'm not suggesting that we should run out and chest bump every day before we go to our desks. But I am saying that if you have some quiet, maybe private, thing that you do to get your day started, you might be a little bit better at it.

So a lot of what athletes and performers do is about reducing their pregame jitters. But isn't some amount of anxiety supposed to help you amp up for a big moment?

Yeah, no question. I was not a very good high school athlete. And when I started this reporting, I thought a lot of this was about adrenaline and about getting yourself psyched up, amped up, highly energized. The more research I did, the more I found out that that's really a simplistic view.

Adrenaline is a physiological response. But it's much more about what you're feeling, and it's about reducing your anxiety, trying to boost your confidence, and trying to manage your energy level so that it's appropriate to what you're trying to do. If you're a WWE wrestler, that's a little bit different than giving a commencement address. So you need to calibrate the energy level to make sure it's right for what you're doing.

What about trying to increase your confidence, though? I mean, can these rituals and things really help with that? Or is it like the movie Dumbo, *where little Dumbo had that silly feather and thought that's how he could fly? Is it just that this helps me because I believe it helps me?*

Yeah, so the feather would be an example of a superstitious ritual because clearly the feather doesn't really help him fly. It's just a placebo effect. What can help you gain confidence is controlling your thought patterns and thinking about what I'd call your greatest hits. So, Sarah, for the show, if you were going to get yourself psyched up, you should think about the best podcast interviews you've done. You might actually want to go back for five minutes at your desk and listen to a couple of them.

Before I walked in the room with you today, I went back and listened to the best interview I've had with you because it made me think, gosh, you're good at this. And that's what you want to be thinking before you go into these environments. It sounds cheesy. You may remember the Stuart Smalley self-affirmations from *Saturday Night Live* in the '90s: "I'm special . . . People like me." But it does work. The messages there are to be relentlessly upbeat and positive. Be confident. Remember your greatest hits. And basically talk yourself up and psych yourself up with the idea that you've done this before, and you can do it again.

Was there any organization you came across where they really do make you go back and actually listen or watch your greatest hits?

At the U.S. Military Academy at West Point, I spent a day in what they call the Center for Enhanced Performance, which is a team of psychologists that work at West Point. And one of the things they do is take their athletes and their cadets and put them in these enclosed, almost egg-shaped chairs. And they play audio tracks that they've created for each cadet that talk about how great they are.

The one I watched was a lacrosse goalie, and there's a professional actor narrating along with music: "John, you're the best lacrosse goalie ever. Remember the game against Shrewsbury High when you did this." So it really is a greatest-hits kind of thing. That's probably the most tangible, visceral example I have found of that.

Could it ever work so well that you'd get to a point where you were insanely overconfident and then that would actually lead you to perform worse?

Sure, I think in a sports setting or in a business setting, we certainly see examples of organizations that become overconfident, too convinced of their dominance, too complacent. But I think for your average, everyday business performers thinking about a job interview, a pitch scenario, a big presentation, or a negotiation, probably the average person suffers a little bit too much from a lack of confidence or an imposter syndrome. On the whole, most people are going to benefit from trying to dial it up a little bit.

One of the things in the book that really surprised me was the part where you explain that golfers who used Tiger Woods's clubs or clubs they were told were Tiger Woods's clubs—I'm not sure he participated in the study—actually golfed better than players who were just using any old random club. How does something like that work?

They call that process "social contagion," and it's the theory that knowing that someone celebrated or highly accomplished has touched an object physically imbues some magical powers. I tried to test that out in the book. I reached out to Malcolm Gladwell, who's a very well-known and acclaimed nonfiction writer. I asked him if I could write the book on a keyboard that he had used. Knowing that such a great writer has typed on these same keys and struggled through it absolutely helped me. I don't know if Tiger Woods's club would help my golf game though. My golf game is really beyond help. [Laughter]

Yes, I've actually read about similar studies—I'm not sure how good they are—that show that when women wear heels, they feel more confident. I think in my case, the opposite is true, because I have a really hard time walking in heels. But that's something where if you are Stephen Colbert or David Ortiz or one of these big stars you talk about in the book, you can really control your environment so that you can perform the ritual. But I think for most of us in offices, it feels like we're not in control of our space. So how can those of us who are not David Ortiz or Stephen Colbert really carve out time for these rituals that are so powerful?

They don't have to be super-elaborate, and they don't have to be something that anyone else can even recognize you're doing. So I don't do this every day, but I'll put on a pair of noise-canceling headphones. That has a functional purpose because it blocks out noise, but also the feel of it on my head is a signal to myself that it's time to get to work here. Some of it is just this Pavlovian signal to our bodies that, OK, it's time for me to get to work. So it doesn't need to be throwing chalk dust in the air or crazy hand gestures. It can be something as simple as putting something on.

That reminds me of the podcast interview that you did with Jerry Seinfeld. I actually think we have a little bit of him talking about that.

Jerry Seinfeld: My routine is to look at notes when my tour producer says five minutes. I put on the jacket. When the jacket goes on, it's like my body knows, OK, now we got to do our trick. And I like to just walk back and forth. That's it. But that's my little preshow routine, and I never vary it. And that seems to just signal everything, and I don't know, it just feels comfortable.

Seinfeld is a great example of how these rituals don't need to be super-elaborate or obvious. These rituals can be fairly simple, but they can still be effective.

One of the people you profile in the book I thought was really interesting was the surgeon who has a whole routine. Tell us a little bit about that guy.

His name is Mark McLaughlin, and he's a brain and spinal surgeon who operates in New Jersey. In high school, he was a very good wrestler. Part of the reason he was so successful as a wrestler was he worked with a sports psychologist to come up with a routine for what he did in the last few minutes before he wrestled. It involved visualization and a lot of the other kind of techniques we've been talking about.

He ended his wrestling career and went to med school. He began to specialize in neurosurgery. As he got into the operating room, he realized this is a lot like wrestling in the sense that it's very high pressure. If things go wrong, they can go very wrong. So he incorporated this same process; he has a set of rituals he does; he has certain kinds of music he listens to. He's very intentional about how much caffeine he has to keep himself alert and to maintain the right level of energy. And he's a great example of the kind of person who says, I need a process the same way I did back when I was an athlete, and if I do these four or five things before I perform every day, I'm going to be better at it.

How did that fit into his workplace?

I've watched him operate. Before he operates, he pushes a chair into a corner of the locker room, puts his iPhone on his chest, listens to Bach, and takes three or four minutes. The nurse comes and gets him as soon as the patient's ready to go, and he's quiet when he scrubs.

Another thing he does is keep an old set of operating equipment, surgical tools, on the tray that he never uses because they belonged to the person who trained him, and he just feels better knowing that he has this piece. It's sort of like the Malcolm Gladwell keyboard. It's this superstition that if it's there, it's like my mentor's in the room with me. So a lot of the stuff is not as obtrusive as you might think it is.

Was there any other time when you were a human guinea pig, testing out these theories on yourself as you worked on the book?

One of the chapters in the book, which is the focus of the HBR article, is on pep talks. While I was reporting that, I was also coaching a Little League team. I definitely didn't go crazy giving Rockne-style speeches to a group of 10-year-olds. But I did become a little bit more intentional and had more of a plan about what I was going to say before and after a game.

When it comes to pep talks, one of the big takeaways is that someone should be very intentional about whether they're trying to give strategy and information or trying to evoke emotion. And so I did. I tried to come up with something that I would say to these Little Leaguers that would boost their confidence before a game. So that's one area where there was a little bit of a guinea pig action.

Did they at any point realize that you were experimenting on them? Or did they just see this as the pep talk that coach always gives us?

No, they're 10 years old. I think the challenge there, and I think it's a good point, is you can get away with it with 10-year-olds. I also have a 16-year-old, and I wouldn't get very far. The moment my older children see me going into anything resembling a pep talk, say, if I'm driving them to the driver's test, they just tell me to shut up. It's more of a challenge with a group like that.

You've mentioned that it was important to decide whether you're trying to convey emotion or explain some kind of tactical strategic thing. What else do people really need to do when they're trying to give a good pep talk?

Deciding between those two tactics is really important, and that research comes out of studies of athletic pep talks. There's some research that looks at whether anger can be a useful motivating force. And there's some that says that you can't use it all the time, but if you're usually fairly calm when you're talking to your team or your subordinates, and every once in a while you do flare up a bit, that can actually have an effect. So that's one tool that a manager or a coach might keep in their arsenal.

The other thing I did was go to Yelp, the online review organization. They have a very large sales force. They make their money by selling ads to local pizza parlors, beauty salons, mechanics, and the like. I went there on the last day of the month. They sell two or three times as many ads on the last day because they're struggling to make their quota. I watched the sales chief give the pep talk in the morning.

She talked for about 20 minutes; I transcribed it and sent it off to some academics who study this. They said she did exactly what the theory suggests. She gave a lot of directions, was very specific about what they should be doing. She was very empathetic, which is another thing you're supposed to do in pep talks. Acknowledge that what you're asking your team to do is hard, and acknowledge that they're doing a good job and that you're thankful for it. And the third element is what I call meaning making, which is trying to connect the task that they're doing every day to some larger purpose for the organization.

We actually recorded a little bit of that, so maybe we could listen to that right now.

> [Excerpt from *Yelp Pep Talk*]:
>   Subject: Team Mary Davis, 104% of quota.
>   [APPLAUSE]
>   Team Roburn hit quota. They're currently sitting at 101%.
>   [APPLAUSE]

So there she's acknowledging the real star performers. She then goes on to connect what those stars did with what everybody could do. She makes the point that you wouldn't have gotten hired here if you couldn't do the same job that that person did. You've all been trained the same. You have the same resources. Just in the same way that Sarah did it, you can do it, too. It's a very effective tactic that people can learn to do in these speeches.

So when you're trying to give someone a pep talk, part of the reason it could be effective is because they would have faith in you. But it does seem like it could very easily become sort of a joke.

Absolutely, and *The Office* has parodied it very well. There's all sorts of great parodies of pep talks online. The success of it comes back to this meaning-making element that the academics talk about. The reason that the pep talks on *The Office* are so ridiculous is that the people working there really don't care about the overall mission of the organization. They don't think the work they're doing is making the world a better place. If you're on a team where you really do care about what the organization or the team is trying to do and you do believe in the cause, then it's a little bit easier to connect the tasks that you're presenting to the team with this larger mission.

Right. Would it work even if the mission was just, we all want to make a lot of money? Would that be enough of a mission to make it work?

Clearly it does in the sense if you look at *The Wolf of Wall Street*; there's a big pep talk in that movie. At the end of the day, all those people were doing was trying to make money, and they were doing it pretty unethically. One of the examples that the academics in the HBR article give is what if you were the assistant manager at a fast-food franchise trying to give a pep talk to a bunch of high school students who are working part-time there. Do they really believe in the work that they're doing? No, they're doing it to get a little bit of work experience, to have some pocket money.

In those cases, you really do have to make the case about where our interests are aligned, because by helping the company do well, you'll make money, and your jobs will be more secure, and we can hire more people. It definitely does take some creativity. I mean, it's one thing if you work for a company that's trying to cure cancer. It's another if you're doing something that's not quite as socially helpful as that.

Are there other things that, as a coach or manager, you could do if you feel there's an employee on your team who's just not focused or who isn't bringing enough energy to work to try to psych them up a little bit?

Sure, when we think of pep talks or locker room speeches, partly because of movies, the image that comes up is one person speaking to a whole room full of people. At Yelp, the sales chief gave a 20-minute speech to 600 salespeople. But then she spent the whole rest of the day going around desk by desk, one on one, reinforcing and empathizing and talking about very specific things: "OK, Sarah, you're about to call an auto mechanic and try to make a sale. Well, here are a couple of things to keep in mind with that space and how to sell."

So what we think of as coaching is really just the one-on-one version of a pep talk, and I think the same things come to mind. Try to build confidence. Try to be empathetic. Try to do things that make people less anxious than they might be. Those are all things that good managers do every day. Just try to come up with a formula or a strategy to specifically accomplish that.

And maybe suggest that they perform a little ritual before they open their email inbox or something.

It definitely can't hurt.

Dan, thank you so much for coming on today.

Thank you, Sarah. This is fun.

And go get 'em, and go sell some books. Sorry. [Laughter] That was awful.

That was great.

I won't do any more pep talks. That's Dan McGinn. He's a senior editor at Harvard Business Review. *He wrote the book* Psyched Up, *and his article "The Science of Pep Talks" is in the July–August 2017 of* Harvard Business Review. *You can find it at HBR.org. Thanks for listening to the HBR IdeaCast. I'm Sarah Green Carmichael.*

Originally published as an HBR IdeaCast, June 29, 2017.

Soulcycle's CEO on Sustaining Growth in a Faddish Industry

by Melanie Whelan

I HAVE A RULE: Whenever I hear about something from three people, I need to give it a try. In 2008 I heard about SoulCycle from a few friends. At the time, it was two years old and had just one studio, on the Upper West Side of Manhattan. I was immediately curious. I loved group fitness classes, and I was a consistent runner, but I didn't Spin. I had tried indoor cycling a few times and hadn't enjoyed it. My friends promised that this studio was different.

It was. First, the studio was tucked away at the end of a long hall. A subtle grapefruit scent emanated from the doorway. The class was packed, but somehow I felt both alone and bonded with the other riders. Every song on the playlist was a remix or a killer mashup of two songs I loved. The instructor was charismatic and authentic. Her energy, and the passion in the room, were contagious. The class was actually fun. Afterward, riders mingled in the lobby with flushed faces, lingering much longer than the tiny space would seem to encourage. It was clear that this was more than just a fitness studio—SoulCycle was a full sensory experience with an engaged community of superfans. One ride in, I understood why and how the buzz of this tiny uptown business could grow.

In 2012 I joined SoulCycle full-time to develop and lead the company's operations, and in 2015 I became CEO. In both those roles my goal has been to see how far we can grow the business and the brand. When I first joined the team, we believed that SoulCycle had the potential to operate 20 or 25 locations concentrated in U.S. coastal cities. Today we have 74 studios, and we've been steadily growing by about 15 locations a year in noncoastal cities such as Chicago, Dallas, Austin, and Houston. We just opened our first international studio, in Toronto. We now know we have a long runway for growth.

As we expand, we stay acutely aware of a potential pitfall: The performance of the fitness and wellness industries tends to be cyclical. That's true for workouts, and it's true for diets. This is a space where things may come and go, and trends may disappear entirely. You can probably think of examples: Jazzercise and Tae Bo and a continual stream of short-lived at-home fitness products—the kinds typically sold on infomercials. Some workouts just repeat the same thing again and again; fatigue, boredom, or distraction sets in, and people decide to try something new. Our challenge is to ensure that SoulCycle never falls into this trap.

We don't think of ourselves as a fitness company; we're a player in the broader experiential economy. I've found that our smartest decisions come from understanding and connecting with our customers. The best testing ground for growth is within the walls of our mirrored studios. We recruit and train our instructors quite differently from the way other fitness companies do, for one major reason: Their role is crucial to our riders' experience. Our instructors are inspirational coaches who leave riders more empowered on their bikes and in their lives. We count on them to make every class unique, to localize the experience, and to connect with different demographic groups. We count on them to inspire in hundreds of thousands of riders every month the same things I felt during my first ride, nearly a decade ago.

Build an Experience

My career in corporate development began at Starwood Hotels in 1999, and it was an exhilarating time. The company had just acquired the Sheraton and Westin brands and launched the W brand. I worked on brand strategy, corporate finance, and real estate acquisitions. It was incredible training for developing an experience-first approach. We rethought the function and feel of a hotel's public spaces. We piped in handpicked playlists, tweaked the lighting, and created just the right energy and vibe to attract and appeal to the local community as much as the guests upstairs. From Starwood, I went to the Virgin Group, where I spent four years working on the launch of Virgin America. We scrutinized our onboard experience. We explored ways to surprise and delight travelers and to offset rudimentary inflight frustrations. In 2007 I joined Equinox as the vice president of business development to help expand the country's most comprehensive fitness brand: personal training, a spa, a boutique, and group exercise under one roof.

In 2010 the CEO of Equinox met with SoulCycle's founders, Julie Rice and Elizabeth Cutler. With just five studios at the time, they needed a partner to keep growing. In Equinox they found expertise in real estate acquisition and operations. By 2016 Equinox held a 97% stake in the company. Through the process, I spent a lot of time with Julie and Elizabeth, focusing on maximizing the brand's potential while maintaining its unique culture. In 2012, nine months after Equinox's first investment, I joined SoulCycle full-time.

My experience in the hotel industry couldn't have better prepared me. From the beginning, Julie and Elizabeth viewed SoulCycle as a hospitality company, with the workout just one dimension of the brand. Our most passionate riders talk more about relationship building and connecting with instructors and other riders than they do about the exercise itself. Leaving a dark studio, sweaty and wearing Spandex, and walking into a bright and crowded lobby breaks down barriers and makes it easier to have real conversations. For many people, friendships made at SoulCycle are the beginning of bigger changes in their lives. They start eating better. They prioritize sleep. Very organically, they plug into a more positive lifestyle. Aspiration becomes reality.

Our studios also differ from traditional fitness classes in the way people value the experience. At a gym you can take unlimited Spinning classes as part of a basic membership. At SoulCycle we don't charge monthly fees, but each class costs $30 to $35, and we ask our riders to book bikes in advance. We believe the pay-per-class model inspires a different level of energy and commitment that contributes to the overall experience.

Our Greatest Asset

"Calories burned" is just a piece of what we deliver to our riders. Measurability matters, but we've heard repeatedly that our team is what keeps riders coming back. We use behavioral interviewing and on-the-job shadowing to ensure that our teams are motivated to make the time a rider spends at one of our studios the best part of the day. It's simple but intuitive: Inspired people want to encourage inspiration in others.

Our instructors are our greatest asset. They take riders on a 45-minute physical, emotional, and musical journey that's similar to theater. You could take a class with the same instructor multiple times in a week, and each experience would be different. Autopilot isn't an option. Lighting, playlists, words of encouragement—everything is customized in real time to the group of riders in the room. The one constant is the incredible physical challenge.

To recruit superstar instructors, we prioritize great personality and individual expression—our training program will fill in any Spinning-specific gaps. To retain those stars, our model values career trajectory. We pay above-market wages, and 78% of our instructors work at SoulCycle full-time, with health insurance, paid vacations, and continuing education, which is very unusual in this industry. (They also have free access to on-staff physical therapists.) Our retention rate over the past few years has exceeded 95%. We get about 20 applications for each opening in our training program. Instructors go through a rigorous 12-week training at our New York headquarters, where they learn everything from the elements of the workout to musicality to anatomy and biomechanics. Once they're on the podium, we invest considerably in further training and development. Because we're a growth company, they see how they can build careers with us by relocating to new markets, growing into regional development roles, or through promotion.

What Makes Us Unique

Soon after I became CEO, we set our sights on going public. But the stock market had other plans. As the financial climate changed, we opted to stay private, partly because the company's solid financial footing didn't require us to rush into the public market. As we prepared for a potential road show, I was peppered with questions about the appeal and sustainability of our brand. One I heard frequently was: "Why are people so obsessed with SoulCycle—and how do you know they'll stay obsessed?" It was a great opportunity for me as a new CEO to consider their concerns and figure out how to address them.

When SoulCycle launched, the boutique fitness industry wasn't well established. Arguably, we created the space. Now competitors are opening Spin, boot camp, and other hybrid-format studios in a fragmented market. We don't pay a lot of attention to other companies in the indoor-cycling or general fitness space, but competition does challenge us to innovate and reconnect with the needs of core customers—our strongest brand ambassadors.

Some of the best lessons come from outside our industry. We consider how Disney trains its staff and how Starbucks keeps its stores community oriented. We watch how Airbnb adds digital products while remaining intuitive. SoulCycle enthusiasts will tell you that it's not just one or two things that make us unique—it's the combination of many. It's the welcoming attitude of the staff, the charisma of our instructors on the podium, our clothing collection, and even our website. It's difficult for imitators to copy any of that, let alone all of it.

We do keep a lookout for blatant copycats that infringe on our intellectual property. If we believe that a studio is truly trying to make customers think they're at a SoulCycle, we pursue a resolution. We found one studio outside North America that looked exactly like our Manhattan studios, with our logo and the same mantra on the wall.

Great Moments in Group Exercise

Some group exercises become popular and stay popular. Others run out of steam. A sampling:

1980s: Jazzercise
Created in 1969 by Judi Sheppard Missett, a Northwestern University under-grad who taught jazz dance on the side, Jazzercise reached peak popularity in the 1980s. Today it has 8,300 franchises, utilizes pop music, and incorporates moves from kickboxing.

1990s: Tae Bo
Tae Bo originated when the U.S. fitness guru Billy Blanks created a workout in his basement while playing the *Rocky* soundtrack. By 1992 he'd launched an exercise video that became one of the decade's most popular infomercials and has sold millions of copies. Blanks is still producing Tae Bo videos, but he's been eclipsed by Beachbody, a company best known for the P90X workout.

2000s: Zumba
The fitness instructor Alberto Pérez was teaching aerobics in Cali, Colombia, one day in the mid-1990s when he forgot his usual workout tapes. He grabbed salsa and merengue music and improvised, and the Latin-infused dance movement was born. In 1999 he took it to Miami; by 2002 he'd trademarked the name Zumba and was selling DVDs on infomercials. Zumba classes would eventually be taught in 200,000 locations worldwide.

We pursued the owners aggressively but appropriately, and the studio made changes.

It's never been part of our strategy, but we've attracted an influential clientele, especially in New York and Los Angeles. Some people think that relying on celebrities to create buzz is its own form of faddishness. There's no question that celebrities have brought us attention, but we don't do anything special to bring them in. From what we hear, high-profile customers appreciate that they can ride in a community setting and that our instructors will never draw attention to them. Michelle Obama rode with us in 2014, when we opened a new studio in Washington, DC. I knew she was there, but we didn't change anything. She seemed to enjoy being one of 60 people, riding a bike to an amazing playlist, sweating a lot, and pushing herself . . . just like the rest of us. Soon she was coming in a couple of times a week.

Location, Location

Choosing the right location for a new studio is a science, and we begin our research a year before we hope to break ground. There's no substitute for spending time locally and hearing from our future riders what matters to them. What do they do with their free time? Where do they exercise and when? What gets them out of bed early? By understanding their lifestyles, we can build a studio around them—not the other way around. And, of course, we consider which of our instructors can best help build community in a new market.

When we look at real estate, we're pretty adaptable. Our studios are 2,500 to 3,500 square feet—a fairly small footprint, so we can go into spaces that wouldn't work for traditional retailers. We care about parking, but we don't need to be on main streets, because we've become a destination. Over time we've also become a desirable brand for landlords, because we bring in traffic and an energy that can complement some of their other tenants. As a result of our disciplined process and approach, we've gotten all our location decisions right so far: Never in the company's history have we closed a studio.

Extending Our Brand

When it comes to innovation, we do some things you might expect. We're always looking to improve the design of our studios, which some people have compared to Apple stores. For instance, we put iPhone chargers inside the lockers, because the charging stations we used to offer at the front desk were getting crowded. This year we plan to introduce our next-generation bikes, which use magnetic resistance and a carbon belt drivetrain. They're superior to our current bikes, which use friction-style resistance: They ride more smoothly, and they last longer. We redesigned the handlebars to accommodate our choreography and to provide greater stability for the upper-body workouts we do on the bikes. And our workout continues to evolve as our riders become stronger. Today our instructors utilize more interval training in their classes, and our hand weights are heavier than they were a few years ago.

We're also expanding our apparel and other categories. After Julie and Elizabeth launched the first SoulCycle studio, they had $2,000 left, so they had T-shirts printed. The first batch sold out in 24 hours. Last year we introduced 14 apparel collections, each a combination of performance and lifestyle pieces—the kind of clothing you can wear outside the studio too. In our most firmly established studios, revenue growth from merchandise exceeded revenue growth from riding in 2016. People wear our logo as a badge of honor, telling the world that they belong to this community.

We've also continued to widen our demographic. When SoulCycle first opened, our riders were almost entirely women from Manhattan's Upper West Side. By 2015, when we were considering an IPO, nearly 80% of our revenue came from locations in New York, Los Angeles, and San Francisco. Today less than 50% comes from those cities, and our clientele varies according to location and time of day. A typical "rooster" class—what we call our 6 AM ride—may be at least 50% men. Some studios offer a teen class at 4 PM. We encourage our instructors to create the right vibe to make every group feel welcome.

We're Not a Fad

I'm confident that we'll keep growing, because people are looking for places to connect with one another and disconnect from technology. They want experiences more than they want stuff. The reason so many wellness categories are growing is that people recognize the importance of investing in their bodies and their minds. That's why we believe that SoulCycle isn't as sensitive to the economy as some other premium brands are. Transitions have proved to be times when our brand is acutely relevant to our customers. Although we were much smaller during the Great Recession, we found that our riders needed us then as a sanctuary and an escape. Similarly, our business increased in the weeks after the 2016 presidential election, which was an uncertain and emotional time for many people. If the economy slows, people may spend less on travel or restaurants, but they'll keep investing in themselves—and we believe they'll keep coming to SoulCycle.

Simply put, we're not a fad. Indoor cycling has been around for more than 30 years because it's a safe and efficient way to get a cardio workout. It's easier on the joints than many other forms of exercise, so riders can stay with us for years. Our founders took this old form of exercise and reinvented it as a full-body workout with emotional and mental benefits that go far beyond fitness. A neon sign that hangs in one of our New York City locations captures who we are: "Pack. Tribe. Crew. Community. Soul." That's how we describe one another, and our riders apply those words to themselves. A first-timer could see that message, glowing from the studio's back wall, and feel a sense of invitation.

Friendships and communities are enduring. Because SoulCycle has those elements at its core, our brand will endure too.

Originally published in July–August 2017. Reprint R1704A

An Interview with Kareem Abdul-Jabbar

Kareem Abdul-Jabbar, *one of the most celebrated players in basketball history, was a natural leader on the court. But the head coaching jobs he later aspired to eluded him. More recently he has become a successful writer, historian, and filmmaker, producing several well-received books and a documentary about unsung African-American heroes.*
Interviewed by Alison Beard

HBR: *Which is more important—talent or practice?*

   Abdul-Jabbar: I think that to really excel, you need both. But a good work ethic trumps lazy talent every time. Conditioning and preparation are key aspects for any competition. My talent would not have lasted as long as it did without them. But I know I was blessed with natural gifts. So I've always felt that the two need to be paired.

You've worked with many coaches over the years, including the great John Wooden at UCLA. What were the most important lessons you learned from them?

   Preparation. It was something that Coach Wooden stressed very emphatically. I trained with Bruce Lee for a while, and it was the same deal. Being prepared, having a good understanding of your own strengths and limitations, and having a good game plan: Those are essential elements of success. Coach Wooden was also an English teacher and a big poetry buff, so it was great to have a relationship with a man who was so multifaceted and such an excellent mentor.

In the NCAA and the NBA you occasionally faced racism. How did you play through those distractions?

If you let it distract you, you're playing into their hands. Their whole purpose is to distract you and prevent you from succeeding. And for me, success was the goal. My success and the success of other black Americans was exactly what would silence people who indulged in racism. So it was "Keep your eyes on the prize." That was one of the messages of the civil rights movement, and I tried to do it.

You were known as a focused player who wasn't very personable. Did that hurt your career?

Well, it had a negative effect on how I was portrayed. But I had no one to explain the value of public relations to me. When I was in college, there was such an intense demand from the press that John Wooden said they couldn't talk to me at all. So that was what I took for normal going into the NBA. Being at the top of my game and working as hard as I could for the people who employed me— that was my primary focus, and everything else was secondary. So I didn't always respond to social situations in a pleasant way. When it came to talking to people, I was kind of reserved. But shyness is something you have to overcome. Later in my career, I started doing a lot better relating to fans and talking to the media. I think that's continued to improve in my retirement.

Do you enjoy it now? Or do you still grit your teeth?

Well, let me say this: It doesn't bother me anymore. I can handle it. A lot of the people in the media are good people, and by being more accessible, you get to find that out. It's just like being in any marketplace. There are good people and thieves. And you've got to have the judgment to understand which is which and adjust.

What did you learn from your teammates?

You learn to appreciate them, because you can't win by yourself. One person can't get it done. So you appreciate the guys who put in the hard work and don't necessarily get the accolades or the big paycheck, but they're the guys who make it possible for you to shine and for the team to shine.

There's a funny story about the end of your first game with Magic Johnson.

What happened was I made the winning shot, and it was like he had just won a championship. He was going crazy, wrestling me down and hugging me and everything. When we got in the locker room, I said, "Look, we've got 81 more games to play." So he got the message from me that it was a long haul, and if you're going to ride the emotions that intensely, you'll be a wreck. But from him, in that same moment, I learned that it's OK to have some fun and enjoy things as you're having the experience. You can't be so totally about brass tacks that you don't enjoy the smaller successes that of course lead to bigger and better things.

As a captain, how did you motivate other players?

By example. I was always in shape. I was always a team player. I understood the fundamentals of the game and worked on them constantly, during the season and in the off-season. And I tried to be always prepared and focused.

What about "managing up" to your coaches?

I was fortunate to have very good coaches who knew what they were doing. But if I had a suggestion, I would try to convey it in a respectful way. Respect always makes people more amenable to criticism or a correction. The whole idea of mutual appreciation really smooths out those interactions between people on different levels.

You played until you were 42. How did you avoid burnout?

I just thought that I had the greatest job in the world, wouldn't last forever. In one of my books I quote Jackie Robinson saying "Athletes die twice." When you no longer have what it takes to play professional sports, that's a death of sorts. So I knew that was coming.

But I tried to be at my best for as long as I could, and I enjoyed the competition.

You've done some coaching work since your retirement. How difficult is the transition from player to coach?

I don't think it's a difficult transition, because all the people who criticize—the management and the media—focus on the players. You have to do some really obvious things as a coach for them to focus on you. So being out of the bull's-eye helps.

I read one interview in which you said you had this vast body of knowledge in your head, you knew the game inside and out, but the trick was to figure out how to communicate that. So what's the secret?

You have to be patient. Talented young athletes always think that they've got it all figured out. And they don't. You never do. People who have played the game and have experience—they know things that can help you. Dealing with cocky players who don't feel that they have anything to learn—that's a tough job. Dealing with players who don't have that attitude is much easier. In any coaching situation you'll find a mixture. So you've got to be flexible. You've got to understand personalities, what motivates people, how to break through the things that make people stubborn and unwilling to try new things.

Are you disappointed that you never became a head coach in the NBA or the NCAA?

When I first tried to do some coaching, I was approaching 50. So I was advanced in years to be a rookie. And then the whole lack of being social—my reputation as a difficult person—might have scared people off. It's been disappointing at times, but I've had some successes, most recently with Andrew Bynum at the Lakers. He was 17 years old when I started working with him, and had not played a lot of basketball. He made great strides because he had a great attitude, and I think I was able to make him a very valuable member of our team. I kind of hang my hat on that situation.

Tell me about your transition to working as a writer, a historian, and a filmmaker.

I didn't really see it as a transition. I was probably those things, certainly a writer and a historian, when I was in grade school. I used to get good grades in English and history because I enjoyed writing. So I had that foundation to call upon, and it's been a very rewarding part of my life, especially after having one career that had nothing to do with it. With the filmmaking, I've always been a movie fan, because my mom was. She would take me to all the classic films in the '50s. And at UCLA, I worked for a film company for three summers. Mike Frankovich, a UCLA alumnus, was at Columbia Pictures, and he gave me a job.

Could you get people to take you seriously right away?

Many athletes make grandiose statements, and very rarely do they follow through. So I imagine most people were waiting for the proof. But the proof came pretty quickly. My first history book, *Black Profiles in Courage*, made the *New York Times* best-seller list. But the best reward was teachers in inner cities telling me the book made it possible for them to figure out their black-history lesson plans.

I know you recently battled leukemia. How has that changed your perspective?

When you face something that could be life threatening, it makes you really appreciate the good things in your life. I'm in total remission now, and the doctors say that if I continue to do what they tell me to do, I'm going to continue to hang around. So I feel very fortunate, and it makes me appreciate every day even more.

Did that take resilience of a different sort from what you needed playing basketball?

No—actually, I think it was more or less the same. I thought I was in a life-or-death situation, and just like everything else, you've got to go into it prepared. That really helped calm me down. I was going to face it calmly and do the best I could.

You have five children. What advice have you given them about their careers?

Well, the very first thing is be educated. My youngest is in college now, and the other four all have their degrees. And then I've just told them to follow their hearts, their instincts.

What would you like to be remembered for?

I know I'll be remembered for the things I did on the basketball court. But I hope people will also see that, with my books and my film, I was multidimensional, and somebody who should be respected.

Originally published in January–February 2012. Reprint R1201Q

Major League Innovation

by Scott D. Anthony

IT'S OCTOBER, AND IF you're an American sports fan, you're probably choosing sides in the upcoming World Series—the culmination and champion crowner of Major League Baseball's seven-month season. But are you reflecting on what you as a manager could learn from the winning team?

When you think about it, a corporate executive on the hook for delivering growth-fueling innovation has much in common with a ball club's general manager. Both are constantly shifting their line-ups, making decisions to add or prune under high degrees of uncertainty. Both have stakeholders demanding immediate results, but also deeply appreciate that history will be the judge of their true legacy. Vindication for wise choices sometimes doesn't come for years, and even the best leaders lose more games than they expect to along the way.

Is it possible that the similarities extend beyond the challenges? Could the ways that general managers *solve* their problems translate to business? In at least three major areas, it seems so. If you're an innovation manager struggling to predict the success of potential new offerings, develop promising ideas, and assemble a balanced portfolio of growth initiatives, the best kind of inspiration may come from the nearest ballpark. (Whether you expense the ticket is your own affair.)

Discover What Really Indicates Success

Famously, the Sabermetrics revolution in baseball (named for its basis in research conducted by members of the Society for American Baseball Research, and described by Michael Lewis in *Moneyball*) has taught general managers and fans how to zero in on the real predictors of performance in the big leagues and the decisions that really win games. As an executive managing a portfolio of innovation initiatives, you need to develop the same willingness to go beyond long-held assumptions and simplistic metrics.

Consider the conundrum presented by Jeff Bagwell and Jeff Ballard, who have little in common other than their given names. The former was a slugging first baseman who had an illustrious career. The latter was a pitcher whose performance was lackluster—save for one sterling season. Obviously, Bagwell would have been the better player to bet on, but could a general manager have predicted that early on?

Not if, as was long the practice, he overlooked minor league statistics. Given the difference between the majors and the minors in level of play, talent scouts traditionally dismissed the outcomes of minor league games as almost meaningless. Instead they looked for fundamentals—the physical attributes and skills that equip a player for high-level competition. Few complained, therefore, when in 1990 the Boston Red Sox traded a 22-year-old Bagwell to the Houston Astros for an aging left-handed reliever. Sure, Bagwell had racked up hits in the minors, but he wasn't much of a third baseman (his position at the time). Worse, he was squat and had an unorthodox swing.

Bagwell went on to slug 449 home runs during his career, and even collected the National League's Most Valuable Player award in 1994. The few students of the game who had seen his potential, such as the baseball historian Bill James, spotted it because they'd devised some simple algorithms to translate minor league statistics into major league equivalents.

Moreover, today's analysts would instantly have recognized that Jeff Ballard's pitching performance in his breakout major league season was an aberration. (Ballard did have superficially good minor league stats, but deeper analysis of his hits allowed, walks, and strikeouts demonstrates that his results came from good defense and luck—not sustainable skill.) Few observers would have agreed as they watched the 25-year-old left-hander lead the Baltimore Orioles—who had lost their first 21 games in the previous season— to the brink of the playoffs. In 1989 Ballard won 18 games, had a 3.43 earned run average, and finished sixth in the Cy Young race for the American League's best pitcher. He went on to win 13 more games . . . in the rest of his career.

The implication for business innovation managers is that a more insightful analysis of available information can overturn orthodoxy and inspire better tactics, investment decisions, and personnel management. Perhaps the scientific approach will never go quite so far in the realm of management; baseball, with its discrete, largely independent events, is particularly well suited to it, and the data to support similar statistical analysis in innovation management simply don't exist.

The innovation manager isn't helpless, however. Research by Clayton Christensen, Robert Burgelman, Vijay Govindarajan, Henry Mintzberg, Rita McGrath, and many others continues to highlight historical patterns of success that can make the market performance of a given innovation more predictable—and that challenge the conventional wisdom about how to choose among competing investment proposals. (See the sidebar "Sizing Up an Innovation's Potential.")

Build Your Organization's Depth Chart

A depth chart reflects a team's level of investment in different areas— the bench strength backing up every position. It signals much about strategic priorities, such as where risks are perceived to be highest and redundancy most necessary. Companies should think in the same ways about their innovation portfolios. Do they have a balance of offensive and defensive strategies? Are they consciously exploring

Sizing Up an Innovation's Potential

INNOVATION MANAGERS, like baseball managers, need to make decisions in new ways.

Old school Responds to the needs of a company's best and most discerning customers.

New school Targets customers left behind by feature-rich offerings or otherwise ignored. Contrast Sony's struggles with the success of firms embracing casual gamers, convenience-seeking camcorder users, and piracy-tolerant MP3 fans. The stats that could have predicted the smash hits Wii, Flip Video, and iPod would have gauged how well they served "overshot" consumers.

Old school Employs proprietary technologies, capitalizing on huge investments in patents to make innovations unassailable.

New school Draws its power from the ingeniousness of the business model. (The iPod and the iPhone, for example, aren't interesting stories without iTunes and AppExchange.) Forgoes patented technology in favor of getting to market before someone else seizes the opportunity.

Old school Focuses obsessively on first-year revenues as the early indicator of potential.

New school Switches the question from "How high were revenues?" to "How low were losses?" Nothing about a slow start says that a business won't get big. First-year revenue of 17 recent disruptive innovators—including Google, Research in Motion, and Netflix—averaged a mere $13.5 million. But tiny first-year losses gave them the freedom and resources to change course as they learned.

---

new channels or geographies? Do they have ideas with meaningfully different strategic intents, such as creating new growth platforms rather than extending current ones, or marketing based on features or functions rather than on packaging and promotion?

Of course, a baseball depth chart begins with what everyone agrees is the right dimension on which the team must be diversified: its player positions. It's impossible to imagine a general manager's saying "I'm really happy with our team's depth—40% of the players are from Latin America, 30% are from Asia, and 30% are from North America." It's obvious to everyone that the real question is whether the team has sufficient coverage of the pitcher's mound, first base, the outfield, and so forth. Further, general managers seek players who throw with different hands and have varying skill bases, such as speed or power.

For corporate managers, what constitutes a usefully diverse innovation portfolio can be less clear. Too often, as they field one close-to-the-core line extension after another, they persuade themselves that they are diversifying, perhaps because the new offerings target quite different consumer segments. Yet these managers may be missing a more important dimension across which they should be spreading their bets. For example, is it wise to design all innovations to move through the same channels? (Could P&G implode if Wal-Mart stopped selling branded products?) Don't be unprepared for what might seem to come out of left field.

Develop Potential in the Minor Leagues

Baseball's farm system holds lessons by analogy: Most professional ball clubs oversee several levels of teams, and even the best prospects spend a few years in the lower levels before heading to "the show."

One rationale for the multitiered system is that talent of a major league caliber isn't always obvious when a player is young. The annual major league draft goes on for dozens of rounds. Although most great players are snapped up in the first few, teams sometimes land talent late in the draft. For example, in 1988 the Los Angeles Dodgers selected Mike Piazza in the 62nd round. Some suggested that he'd been chosen only because his father was a childhood friend of Tommy Lasorda, then the Dodgers' manager. Piazza turned out to be one of the great batting catchers in the history of baseball, hitting 0.308 with 427 home runs in his 16-year career.

Not only does an extensive minor league system allow teams to identify the players with sufficient talent to perform at the major league level, but it allows coaches to work with players to address identified limitations in lower-pressure environments.

Let's apply this analogy to packaged goods companies. For them, making it to the show means scoring scarce shelf space in a large

Develop potential in the minor leagues

	Baseball's minor leagues	Innovation's minor leagues
Rookie league	Expose young prospects to professional competition	Test rough concepts and ideas among employees
Class A	Conduct focused development effort on "high ceiling" prospects	Expose customers to rough prototypes
Class AA	Clearly identify prospects with major league potential	Bring concepts to small-scale transactional environments
Class AAA	Polish prospects in preparation for major league competition	Execute market-facing pilots

retailer like Wal-Mart. Such retailers can be brutally discriminating. If in its first few weeks a new product doesn't appear capable of selling well enough to earn that real estate, its career is over. But research on innovation shows that almost nothing springs perfectly formed from the heads of designers; about the only thing you can count on is that you won't get the strategy right on day one. Exposing ideas to the mass market too early increases both the likelihood of failure and its economic impact. It doesn't provide room for learning to occur.

What would it mean to create a minor league system for product and service innovations? To be sure, companies have long made use of test-market research and regional rollouts. The key is to deliberately organize such activities into a system whereby new offerings face steadily increasing levels of scrutiny from prospective customers and become stronger in the process. Procter & Gamble, for example, has made a recent effort to test very-early-stage ideas in low-stakes but revealing market settings. The company distributed a potentially game-changing baby care product to a handful of consumers at an amusement park and then began selling the product over the internet. It opened a small store in Ohio to test Swash, a line of fabric-care products targeting the 30% of garments that are reworn without being laundered. It opened three stores in Kansas to test the potential of Tide-branded dry cleaners. P&G's chairman, A.G. Lafley, is a strong believer in this kind of staged learning. In a 2008 discussion he told me, "I've become a pretty big believer in getting the idea or technology to some relatively clear concept expression and some relatively crude prototype as fast as you possibly can, and then [getting] that in front of prospective customers." Like any great general manager, he knows not to launch new players into the big leagues without proof points along the way.

Originally published in October 2009. Reprint R0910C

Looking Past Performance in Your Star Talent

by Mark de Rond, Adrian Moorhouse, and Matt Rogan

THE NBA DRAFT has, since 1950, been the means of bringing the cream of college basketball talent into the professional ranks. Pro teams take views and stake fortunes on those college kids most likely to step up successfully.

In 1998, Briton Michael Olowokandi was first pick, drafted to the L.A. Clippers. His selection was big news, not because the soccer-obsessed Britons had finally produced a basketball talent, but because he had only been playing the game for five years, since 1993. Although Olowokandi had only played basketball in the U.K. for two years before his freshman year, coaches at the University of the Pacific were intrigued by his seven-foot frame and recruited him. He had no game to speak of, but huge potential. It was unclear until very late in his college career that he was NBA material, let alone a potential number-one pick.

Sports teams under salary caps rely on balancing performance with potential. American sports in particular have led the world in professionalizing this skill. Michael Lewis's *Moneyball* describes how the Oakland A's used data analysis to understand the trade-off between performance, potential, and player value on the open market. In U.S. pro sports, this cat is now out of the bag. Performance data in itself is now a commodity purchase, so mainstream that Brad Pitt starred in *Moneyball* the movie.

On one level, business is slowly catching on. Well-handled psychometric tests provide not only a currency for assessing personal traits, but also potential fit within an organization. In theory, we finally have an objective view of who our number-one pick should be. In practice, this is no time to be smug. Recent research suggests that 70% of our current crop of high performers in business lack critical attributes essential to success in future roles.[1] We may have all the data in the world, yet we're still not consistently making the right calls.

Why not? Perhaps progress in sports offers a clue. Given that a data-based view of potential versus value is now held by each MLB team, Billy Beane, the brains behind the Moneyball revolution, is thinking differently. He has said, "Data is now only part of the picture. When the competition zigs, I have to zag." While the number crunching still happens, he is also sending his scouts to understand the backgrounds of his prospective draft picks and trades. He wants to meet their parents and their friends, to observe them in the evenings after a defeat. The best soccer managers in England, Alex Ferguson and Arsene Wenger, do the same. They do so because they don't just want a theoretical view of potential; they also want to find clues as to what lies beneath. They want to discover how resilient each talented individual might be, and how prone they could be to derailment.

Professional sports require dedication and performance under pressure. In this environment, personal traits and preferences that manifest themselves as strengths can become counterproductive. Self-belief can become unhelpful ego, which has an impact on the ability to learn from setbacks. A win-at-all-costs mentality can turn into a desire to bend the rules a little too far. Understanding potential derailment minimizes the risk of hiring talented but flawed individuals.

We see this tendency in business too, of course. In his book *Personality and the Fate of Organizations*, Robert Hogan explains, "There are strengths and weaknesses associated with various derailment factors . . . good things taken to the extreme turn into bad things." For example, attention to detail can later turn into a career-limiting desire to micro-manage as opposed to lead an organization. Developing self-awareness is at the root of any successful strategy to deal with derailment. The New York Giants don't just recruit those most likely to cope; they run a program called "Choices, Decisions and Consequences" to help their players proactively understand and manage their own potential causes of derailment.

Business, like sports, is a roller coaster. Success is high profile, failure higher still. Given this, any outlook that fails to recognize the potential threat of derailment and to prize the resilience necessary for coping with setbacks is an incomplete picture. We characterize future potential in terms of three dimensions—commitment, ability, and resilience. Those individuals in sport or business with the highest potential are replete in all three. "Loyal Servants" lack the ability to progress much further but have the commitment and resilience to deliver for the long term. "Prima Donnas" are full of ability and resilience but lack the commitment to stay the course. They can become the stars of the future, but it might not be with you. "Brittle Stars" are full of ability and commitment, but can derail under pressure. They can deliver for you, as long as you provide the necessary support along the way.

Like every team, your business will blend Brittle Stars, Loyal Servants, and Prima Donnas as well as the highest-potential talent. Each group can be supported and challenged to move forward. In that spirit, here are three key insights from sports' top talent developers:

- **Just like the University of the Pacific:** Remember current performance is often a misleading barometer of future potential.

- **Just like Manchester United and Arsenal Soccer Clubs:** Insist on understanding the people behind the data.

- **Just like the New York Giants:** Encourage your talent to understand and actively manage their own personal sources of potential derailment.

Carefully assessing your top talent is more than picking the best of the best. In looking at your team, you can see what your stars bring to the table and prevent the possibility of future derailment.

Originally published on June 2011 on HBR.org.

Note

1. Jean Martin and Conrad Schmidt, "How to Keep Your Top Talent," *Harvard Business Review*, May 2010.

An Interview with Mikhail Baryshnikov

Mikhail Baryshnikov *began studying ballet at age nine in his native Riga, Latvia, then part of the Soviet Union. By his early twenties he had been described by one critic as "the most perfect dancer I have ever seen" and was the star of the famed Kirov Ballet. In 1974 he defected to Canada and then settled in the U.S. at the American Ballet Theatre, where he later became artistic director. He left in 1989 to cofound a modern dance company and take on film, theater, and TV roles. He's now artistic director of the Baryshnikov Arts Center and, at age 63, still performs.* **Interviewed by Alison Beard**

HBR: *Your career has been all about reinvention—classical to modern dance, stage to film to TV, performing to managing and back again. Why?*

Baryshnikov: It's instinctive. There's an internal clock that dictates what interests me at any given time. Change in any person's life is propelled by an almost primal need to explore, to test boundaries. I just follow that urge. In some cases, I look at what others are doing and stubbornly go in the opposite direction. Sometimes it works, sometimes I fail. There are no guarantees.

How hard was the transition to management?

I've had the good fortune to work with very structured dance companies, and I could see early on what a huge responsibility managing one would be. When I took it on, it was a growing-up experience. It forced me to make artistic decisions unrelated to my own career and to think more seriously about creating opportunities for others. I think what I've been best at is sticking to a vision for whatever group I'm leading, making the tough decisions that might not favor the people I like but that make sense for the organization as a whole. When I'm working with other artists I can be an obedient puppy, but in an office situation I like to think I'm the big dog. I don't want to take direction. I haven't always been as patient as I should have been, expecting too much, too fast, and getting frustrated with how long it can take to build support for new ideas. But I'm still learning.

You've worked with the legends of dance—Alexander Pushkin, George Balanchine, Twyla Tharp, Jerome Robbins, Alvin Ailey. What can you tell us about effective mentoring?

I don't consider myself a mentor; I'm more of a cheerleader. But the best lesson from all the people I've worked with is to understand who you are as a person on stage. Whatever new craft you learn has to go through your own psychology, your own body and mind, in order to come out as something revealing and interesting for the audience.

How about effective teamwork?

I've always liked the camaraderie of group performance. To really collaborate, you have to figure out how to work with anyone and give 100%. It's about spitting out your ego and becoming a foot soldier when necessary. The creative process isn't a human rights march. Some things aren't fair. Creators can be temperamental, but they have to be forgiven in this business. If you can't deal with that, you should step out.

You learned 26 new roles in your first two years as principal dancer at the ABT. At the New York City Ballet it was 20 in a year. What's the key to mastering new roles quickly?

There is no one secret. It takes positive energy, talent, a lot of hard work, and a willingness to absorb everything possible from the people you're working with. And some luck surely helps. I don't think I always mastered everything. Sometimes I took on too much. But it was a young person's appetite. In retrospect, I think the failures might have been the most important experiences.

Can you give me an example?

Why are you trying to make me remember things I've worked so hard to forget? Seriously though, failures are the best school you can get. But let's not go into details.

How do you handle pre-performance jitters?

There's no magic pill, but by the time those nerves hit, there's nowhere to go but forward.

You've hinted at retirement. But at 63 you're still dancing. Have you gotten better with age?

I don't know how much longer I'll dance, but I've certainly learned how to pace myself. I'm not sure it's up to me to decide what, if anything, has improved. I can only say that age forces you to pare things down to what's essential.

I've read that you hate critics.

Well, that's an exaggeration. It's just that there's no easy way to be completely objective as a critic. And most artists don't want to be subjected to someone else's opinion of their work anyway.

Do you have an inner critic?

You absolutely have to have one—maybe a whole stable of them.

What type of recognition do you value most?

I don't really put a lot of value on recognition from others. I mean, it's always nice when people are appreciative. If they're still thinking of something they saw me do in a performance somewhere, that's great, but I just try and do my best. That's all I can do.

What have been your most satisfying professional experiences?

Meeting all the bizarre, weird, beautiful people in the arts. They are divinely obsessed, and that has made my life so much more interesting than I could have imagined.

Who has been most inspirational?

I like to kiss, but I don't tell.

You're one of the world's most famous Soviet defectors. Were there positive aspects to the environment you fled? And do you see any downsides to being a performance artist in the United States?

The Soviet system gave me my occupation, my craft. They schooled me, and that is the biggest present a government can give a young person. When I left, I escaped government control over the individual but inherited total responsibility for myself. That wasn't so difficult for me because I was already known and had plenty of opportunities. But performers in the U.S. really have to figure out how to survive, how to refine their talent without much support from government—or from anyone else for that matter. And don't get me started on the lack of government support for arts education in the U.S. But, you know, even with the negatives, I'd still drop my anchor here in this country if I had to make the choice again.

Why is the BAC a cross-disciplinary organization?

The more you see, the more you know, and—hopefully—the better you get. There is this idea that artists shouldn't "pollute" their creative instincts by seeing other artists' work. I think this is wrong. Any place that provides a common ground for artists to learn from one another is a good thing.

Why are you so good at what you do?

Please don't make me think about this. This is the worst thing one can do: sit around and think about how good you've gotten at something. Besides, I'm not always so great—ask my wife.

Originally published in May 2011. Reprint R1105N

How the Best of the Best Get Better and Better

by Graham Jones

UNTIL 1954, MOST PEOPLE BELIEVED that a human being was incapable of running a mile in less than four minutes. But that very year, English miler Roger Bannister proved them wrong.

"Doctors and scientists said that breaking the four-minute mile was impossible, that one would die in the attempt," Bannister is reported to have said afterward. "Thus, when I got up from the track after collapsing at the finish line, I figured I was dead." Which goes to show that in sports, as in business, the main obstacle to achieving "the impossible" may be a self-limiting mind-set.

As a sports psychologist, I spent much of my career as a consultant to Olympic and world champions in rowing, swimming, squash, track and field, sailing, trampolining, and judo. Then in 1995, I teamed up with Olympic gold medal swimmer Adrian Moorhouse to start Lane4, a firm that has been bringing the lessons from elite athletic performance to *Fortune* 500 and FTSE 100 companies, with the help of other world-class athletes such as Greg Searle, Alison Mowbray, and Tom Murray. Sport is not business, of course, but the parallels are striking. In both worlds, elite performers are not born but made. Obviously, star athletes must have some innate, natural ability—coordination, physical flexibility, anatomical capacities—just as successful senior executives need to be able to think strategically and relate to people. But the real key to excellence in both sports and business is not the ability to swim fast or do quantitative analyses quickly in your head; rather, it is mental toughness.

Elite performers in both arenas thrive on pressure; they excel when the heat is turned up. Their rise to the top is the result of very careful planning—of setting and hitting hundreds of small goals. Elite performers use competition to hone their skills, and they reinvent themselves continually to stay ahead of the pack. Finally, whenever they score big wins, top performers take time to celebrate their victories. Let's look at how these behaviors translate to the executive suite.

Love the Pressure

You can't stay at the top if you aren't comfortable in high-stress situations. Indeed, the ability to remain cool under fire is the one trait of elite performers that is most often thought of as inborn. But in fact you can learn to love the pressure—for driving you to perform better than you ever thought you could. To do that, however, you have to first make a *choice* to devote yourself passionately to self-improvement. Greg Searle, who won an Olympic gold medal in rowing, is often asked whether success was worth the price. He always gives the same reply: "I never made any sacrifices; I made choices."

Managing pressure is a lot easier if you can focus just on your own excellence. Top sports performers don't allow themselves to be distracted by the victories or failures of others. They concentrate on what they can control and forget the rest. They rarely let themselves be sidetracked by events outside a competition. World-class golfer Darren Clarke, for example, helped lead the European team to a Ryder Cup victory in 2006, six weeks after the death of his beloved wife. Elite performers are masters of compartmentalization.

If you want to be a high flier in business, you must be equally inner-focused and self-directed. Consider one executive I'll call Jack. When he was a young man, wrestling was his passion, and he turned down an offer from Harvard to attend a less-prominent undergraduate school that had a better-ranked wrestling team. Later, after earning his MBA, Jack was recruited by a prestigious investment-banking firm, where he eventually rose up to the rank of executive director. Even then, he wasn't driven by any need to impress others. "Don't think for a minute I'm doing this for the status," he once told me. "I'm doing it for myself. This is the stuff I think about in the shower. I'd do it even if I didn't earn a penny."

People who are as self-motivated as Jack or Darren Clarke rarely indulge in self-flagellation. That's not to say that elite performers aren't hard on themselves; they would not have gotten so far without being hard on themselves. But when things go awry, business and sports superstars dust themselves off and move on.

Another thing that helps star performers love the pressure is their ability to switch their involvement in their endeavors on and off. A good way to do this is to have a secondary passion in life. Rower Alison Mowbray, for example, always set time aside to practice the piano, despite her grueling athletic-training schedule. Not only did she win a silver medal in the Olympics in 2004, but she also became an accomplished pianist in the process.

For top executives, the adrenaline rush of the job can be so addictive that it's difficult to break away. But unless you are able to put the day behind you, as elite athletes can, you'll inevitably run the risk of burning out. Many leading businesspeople are passionate about their hobbies; Richard Branson is famous for his hot-air balloon adventures, for instance. However, even small diversions such as bridge or the opera can be remarkably powerful in helping executives tune out and reenergize.

Fixate on the Long Term

Much of star athletes' ability to rebound from defeat comes from an intense focus on long-term goals and aspirations. At the same time, both sports stars and their coaches are keenly aware that the road to long-term success is paved with small achievements.

The trick here is to meticulously plan short-term goals so that performance will peak at major, rather than minor, events. For athletes who participate in Olympic sports, for example, the training and preparation are geared to a four-year cycle. However, these athletes may also be competing in world championships every year. The inevitable tension arising from this complicated timetable requires very careful management.

Adrian Moorhouse's Olympic gold medal success in 1988 is a case in point. His long-term goal was to swim the 100-meter breaststroke in a time of 62 seconds, because he and his coach had calculated four years in advance that this time should be good enough to win the gold. Of course, Adrian thought about winning in the interim, but all of his training and practice was geared toward hitting a time of 62 seconds or better in the Summer Olympics in Seoul. He mapped out specific short-term goals in every area that would affect his performance—strength training, nutrition, mental toughness, technique and more—to make sure he achieved that ultimate goal.

Successful executives often carefully plan out their path to a long-term goal too. I once coached a woman I'll call Deborah, an IT manager who worked for a low-budget airline. Her long-term goal was to become a senior executive in three years. To that end, we identified several performance areas in which she needed to excel—for example, increasing her reputation and influence among executives in other departments of the company and managing complex initiatives. We then identified short-term goals that underpinned achievements in each performance area, such as joining a companywide task force and leading an international project. Together we built a system that closely monitored whether Deborah was achieving the interim goals that would help her fulfill her long-term vision. It paid off. Two months short of her three-year target, Deborah was offered an opportunity to head up the $12 million in-flight business sales unit.

Use the Competition

It's common in track-and-field sports for two elite athletes from different countries to train together. I was at a pre-1996 Olympics training camp for the British team where 100-meter sprinter and then current Olympic champion Linford Christie had a "guest" train with him. His training partner just happened to be Namibian Frankie Fredericks, a silver medalist who had been one of the major threats to Christie's Olympic crown.

World champion rower Tom Murray told me just how competing with the best inspired him to higher achievement. Murray was part of a group of 40 rowers selected to train together with the hopes of gaining one of the 14 spots on the 1996 U.S. Olympic rowing team. Because the final team was chosen only two months before the Atlanta games, this meant that the group of 40 trained together for almost four years.

As Murray recalled, one of the last performance evaluations during the final week leading up to the naming of the Olympic team involved a 2,000-meter test on the rowing machine. The 40 athletes took it in four waves of 10; Murray went in the third wave. During the first two waves, 15 rowers set personal best times, and two recorded times that were faster than anyone in the U.S. had ever gone. The benchmark was immediately raised. Murray realized that he needed to row faster than he'd anticipated. He ended up bettering his previous personal best by three seconds and subsequently made the 1996 team.

If you hope to make it to the very top, like Murray, you too will need to make sure you "train" with the people who will push you the hardest. I once coached an executive I'll call Karl. He declined an opportunity to take a position as the second-in-command at a competitor's firm at twice his current salary. Karl passed up what looked like a standout career opportunity because his current company was deeply committed to coaching him and a cohort of other senior executives on how to become better leaders. Karl had a reputation for burning people out, and he realized that if he moved on, he would continue that pattern of behavior. He remained in the same job because he knew that his coach and peers would help him grow and change his ways.

Smart companies consciously create situations in which their elite performers push one another to levels they would never reach if they were working with less-accomplished colleagues. Talent development programs that bring together a company's stars for intensive training often serve precisely such a purpose. If you want to become a world-class executive, getting into such a program should be one of your first goals.

Reinvent Yourself

It's hard enough getting to the top, but staying there is even harder. You've won that Olympic medal or broken that world record or racked up more wins than anyone in your sport. So how do you motivate yourself to embark on another cycle of building the mental and physical endurance required to win the next time, especially now that you have become the benchmark? That is one of the most difficult challenges facing elite performers, who have to keep reinventing themselves.

Consider trampolinist Sue Shotton. I was working with her when she achieved the number one ranking among women in 1983—that is, she was considered to be the best female trampolinist in the world. Yet she had still not won a world championship.

Shotton was determined to capture that title, and she left nothing to chance. She challenged herself constantly by working with specialists such as physiologists, biomechanists, and elite sports coaches who kept her up to date on cutting-edge thinking. She perfected new moves based on video analysis; she tried different ways of boosting her energy based on nutritional intake. Her efforts to find ways of staying ahead of fiercely ambitious competitors paid off when she won the world championship in 1984, becoming the first British woman ever to hold the title.

Shotton had an insatiable appetite for feedback—a quality I have seen in all the top business performers I have worked with. They have a particularly strong need for instant, in the moment feedback. One top sales and marketing director I worked with told me that he would never have stayed at his current position if the CEO hadn't given him relentless, sometimes brutally honest critiques.

If you're like the elite business performers I have coached, you too are hungry for advice on how to develop and progress. One word of caution, however: While it's good to feel challenged, you need to make sure that any feedback you get is constructive. If criticism doesn't seem helpful at first, probe to see if you can get useful insights about what's behind the negative feedback. Get more specifics. You should be able to see concrete improvements in your performance after getting detailed coaching advice.

Celebrate the Victories

Elite performers know how to party—indeed, they put almost as much effort into their celebrations as they do into their accomplishments. I once worked with a professional golfer who, as he worked his way up the ranks to the top of his sport, would reward himself with something he had prized as a young player—an expensive watch, a fancy car, a new home. These were reminders of his achievements and symbolized to him the hard work, commitment, and dedication he had put into golf for so many years.

Celebration is more than an emotional release. Done effectively, it involves a deep level of analysis and enhanced awareness. The very best performers do not move on before they have scrutinized and understood thoroughly the factors underpinning their success. I saw that discipline in the Welsh rugby team, which I advised from 2000 to 2002. After each game, the team members made a special effort to highlight not only what they did poorly but what they did particularly well. They typically split into small groups to identify and discuss the positive aspects of their performance, so that they could focus on reproducing them in the next game. The exercise was a powerful way to build expertise—and self-confidence. Indeed, the most important function of affirming victory is to provide encouragement for attempts at even tougher stretch goals.

In business, where companies are pressed to meet quarterly earnings and stockholders are impatient, managers must consider the timing and duration of the celebration. Dwelling on success for too long is a distraction and, worse, leads to complacency. Celebrate—but push on. Don't get stuck in the rituals of success. At the end of the day, getting to the next level of performance is what celebrating is really all about.

Smart companies know how to manage the tension between celebrating and looking hungrily for their next achievement. One UK mobile telecom provider puts on an annual ball for its people—spending over £1 million a year. The company hires out well-known venues and brings in pop bands to entertain all the employees. But one factor in the company's success is that its managers know that partying comes number nine on the list of top 10 reasons for wanting to win. Like all elite performers, they also know that partying must be deserved. Without victory, celebrations are meaningless.

The Will to Win

As the spectacle of the Olympics unfolds, it will be easy to be captivated by the flawless performance of elite athletes who make their accomplishments seem almost effortless. Such effortlessness is an illusion, though. Even the most youthful star has typically put in countless years of preparation and has endured repeated failures. But what drives all these elite performers is a fierce desire to compete—and win. Even so, most of those participating in the Olympics this summer will walk away from the games without grabbing a single medal. Those with real mettle will get back into training again. That's what truly separates elite performers from ordinary high achievers. It takes supreme, almost unimaginable grit and courage to get back into the ring and fight to the bitter end. That's what the Olympic athlete does. If you want to be an elite performer in business, that's what you need to do, too.

Originally published in June 2008. Reprint R0806H

An Interview with Joe Girardi

Joe Girardi *wrote in a third-grade essay that he wanted to play for the Chicago Cubs and grew up to do exactly that. After retiring from catching, he coached for the New York Yankees and managed the Florida Marlins for one year, at the end of which he was both fired and named National League Manager of the Year. He then replaced his former boss, Joe Torre, as manager of the Yankees. In 2009 he took the team to its 27th World Series championship.* **Interviewed by Katherine Bell**

HBR: *You're famous for being information-driven and analytical in your approach to managing.*

Joe Girardi: I love numbers. You can never give me too many numbers. I believe they tell a story, if you have a large enough sample. I have an industrial engineering degree—a degree in problem solving, basically. But my whole family is math-oriented, and that's always been how I see things.

How do you coach players on when to abandon the plan and listen to their guts?

If you think too much, you fail, because the game happens too quickly. The key is preparation. You tell the player, "Here's the information—now go play." The data has to become instinctual. You can't think about it in the middle of a pitch. Some players have a hard time using information to improve their instincts, and they usually weed themselves out.

When you were catching and you saw a pitcher losing focus, how did you get him back on track?

I would walk out there and say, "Try to change the rhythm a bit. Try to keep it simple." Usually there's one pitch that gets a pitcher back to his mechanics, and you've got to know what it is. When a guy gets traded to the team, you've got to figure out that pitch as quickly as you can.

How did you change your approach from managing a team of rookies to managing one full of stars?

To me, the principles are the same. You have to show faith in your players and lead by example. You ask your players to be prepared mentally and physically, so you have to be prepared. Beyond that, you've got to adapt to the type of players you have. If you've got a home-run-hitting team, you can't make them all base stealers, and vice versa.

When you replaced Joe Torre, how did you go about setting your own direction for the Yankees?

Most people, including Joe, advised me, "Be yourself. Don't try to be somebody else." I had to earn the players' trust. I knew it would take time and I'd have to work very hard at it, because they had been with Joe a long time. I would flat out ask players, "Do you trust me?" One was a little hesitant. I said, "You know what? I'm going to prove you can trust me." And so I had to go out and prove it to him.

What challenges come with being the most successful sports franchise in American history?

The expectation that it's going to be done every year is the biggest challenge. I like that expectation, because it pushes people to a higher level. But it can be hard on players. Everything we do is under a microscope. Every player who goes out there this year is going to have a bad day or a bad week or even a bad month. But it's the overall picture that matters, and that's why the togetherness we have as a team is so important. You can't get caught up in what you hear and what you read. Your value can't come from others. It can't, or you'll be torn up.

Do you ever get bored?

Do games get long? Does the job sometimes become a grind from a physical standpoint? Yeah. But I don't get bored. I love what I do. I love competition and strategy. I love seeing people succeed—you can be losing a game 19–2 and you can still see that.

Originally published in June 2010. Reprint R1006M

Why There Is an *I* in Team

by Mark de Rond

The Old: There is no *I* in team.
The New: There is an *I* in team. And it matters.
The Challenge: To exploit individual qualities while mitigating the risks these same qualities entail.

GOOD SPELLING DOES NOT EQUAL deep thinking. Take that old devil, "there is no *I* in team." When basketball star Michael Jordan, after a run of twenty straight points, snubbed Coach Tex Winter with, "there may not be an *I* in team, but there is in win," he may have been onto something. A basketball team without superstars rarely makes it to the playoffs, let alone the finals. Such star players as Magic Johnson, Larry Bird, Michael Jordan, Kobe Bryant, Tim Duncan, Shaquille O'Neal, Hakeem Olajuwon, and LeBron James have consistently featured in all but one NBA finals series for the last thirty years. In fact, a team with no starting all-star player has less than a 1/100th chance of winning the championship. By comparison, a team with an all-star player raises the odds of winning to 7.1 percent and of making it to the finals to 16 percent.

These odds increase dramatically as the number of star players per team increases. Those teams with pockets deep enough to field two first-team all-star players have a one-in-four chance of winning a championship and better than a one-in-three chance of making the finals. With three all-stars, these odds increase to 39 percent and

77 percent, respectively. And the argument holds even when controlling for a team's winning percentage during the regular season. When it comes to the playoffs, a star player improves his or her team's chances of winning a championship by 12 percent. A superstar with a relatively weak supporting cast fares better than a team with five good players.[1] Love them or loathe them, individuals matter.

So much then for that old devil. While grammatically correct, as a guiding principle, it is flawed and impractical. It downplays the extent to which high-performance teams benefit from variations in talent, in personality, and even in pay. And it diminishes the value of competition between team members. Even those blissful moments of team flow, when mind and matter fuse effortlessly as all are absorbed in the task at hand are more often than not the consequence of individual differences cleverly brought into play by good leadership. The choice of who is in and who is not will have been decided based on the relevance of particularized attributes to an available set of competencies. In sports as in business, it is the *combination* that matters. Even in teams that are greatly interdependent and prize uniformity—think of synchronized swimming or team sprints in cycling—individuality can be a positive differentiator. Besides, no matter how resolute the belief that individuality be completely eradicated, to collaborate effectively remains a matter of personal choice.

Team decisions require individuals to commit to those around them and to be accountable for their own performance to the team. Should they choose to commit, they will only ever do so for their own reasons. As one of Britain's most distinguished coaches, David Whitaker, put it: "If you want an exceptional team, keep your eye on the individual . . . Teams thrive on individual choice and commitment . . . the most powerful teams are made up of individuals who have chosen to work as a team."[2] Having coached hockey teams to Olympic gold and bronze, World and European silver, he deserves to be taken seriously.

Thus, teams begin and end with individuals. This is not an ideological statement. Nor is it a normative one. This book has no intention of lionizing individuals at the expense of teams or of, God forbid, sanctioning egotism. It does not prioritize individual over collective effort (even if some tasks—particularly those that require logical problem solving—are often better done by individuals than teams). It doesn't even go as far as Jordan's gibe. Its perspective is far subtler. To focus on the *I* in teams is to pursue a very specific level of granularity. It is to see the trees for the forest by granting individuals that degree of choice missing in much popular writing on teams. To keep in mind the individual is to emphasize precisely the sorts of issues that are easily lost when considering teams as the primary unit of analysis.

Thus, the chapters in this book [from which this chapter is excerpted] explore each of the following assertions: The qualities that make individuals attractive can make them difficult. The best individuals put together do not necessarily make for the most effective team. Conflict often arises even as people agree on what needs to be done and why, and actively try to coordinate their efforts with those around them. Their productivity depends on who else is involved, and how many of them there are. It can make sense to trade off competence for likability within a team in even technically demanding environments. Competition within teams can be as valuable as collaboration.

The *I* in team also suggests that the key to managing teams lies not just in advanced statistical techniques, skill complementarities, or team bonding but in an appreciation of their *humanity*. When teams work well, it is because, and not in spite, of individual differences. These differences are at once a source of brilliance and tension, leaving teams poised between entropy and synergy, tension and collective genius.

What may appear like picture-perfect teams are then in reality often quite intricate tapestries of distinct characters united by a common goal but forced into a sanctum where trade-off choices must be made between likability and competence; where powerful but conflicting pressures coexist; where one's success hinges on being able to reconcile camaraderie and rivalry, trust and vigilance, the sacred and the profane; and where they end up getting it wrong as often as right.

These teams can feel fragile to those on the inside, even if perfectly functional on the outside. In contrast to popular belief, teams of high performers are not easy places to be. At times, they are anything but harmonious, but then harmony may well be the result, not cause, of superior performance. Workplace teams are even more complex. Businesses rarely have the luxury of focusing on a single team with one clear objective. The composition of the I's in charge of production will invariably be different to the composition of the I's in charge of sales or R&D. Adding to this complexity, sitting on top of these various teams is typically a small team (the executives) charged with understanding, leading, and managing the multiplicity of teams in their business. And the I's inside them.

What Makes Them Good Makes Them Difficult, Too

This chapter and those that follow will try to untangle the tapestry of high-performance teams to identify the true nature of collective performance. They do so by using insights from elite sports, occasionally supplemented by evidence from experiments in social psychology, organizational behavior, and the sociology and economics of sports. The first of these insights is in some ways also the most exasperating: it seems one cannot have one's cake and eat it too when it comes to turning teams of high performers into high performance teams. With few exceptions, the qualities that make individuals as gifted as they are can make them wearisome as team members. They are often extraordinarily focused, with higher-than-usual thresholds for personal discomfort. This is true in sports as much as in business.

Consider, for example, 1940s baseball star Pete Reiser. Known colloquially as "Pistol Pete," he had to be carried off the diamond eleven times in two and a half years of playing in the minors, three in the army, and ten in the majors (with the Brooklyn Dodgers, Pittsburgh Pirates, Cleveland Indians, and Boston Braves). According to W. C. Heinz's 1958 biopic, "nine times Pete regained consciousness either in the clubhouse or in hospital. He broke a bone in his right elbow, throwing. He broke both ankles, tore a cartilage in his left knee, ripped the muscles in his left leg, sliding. Seven times he crashed into outfield walls, dislocating his left shoulder, breaking his right collarbone and, five times, ending up an unconscious heap on the ground."[3] Yet, according to the *New York Herald Tribune's* Bob Crooke, "Pete Reiser was the best ballplayer I ever saw."[4] Reiser would have it no other way. Nor would we.

In the workplace, personal discomfort is rarely of the same muscular variety, limited instead to sleep deprivation, a poor work-life balance, and excess consumption of food or alcohol or both. But occasionally we find extremes here, too. The managing partner of one of the world's largest and most profitable professional services firms who, realizing that his highly successful team of partners experienced a disproportionally high incidence of divorce, decided to retain the services of one of London's top divorce lawyers. Doing so helped mitigate the anxiety and additional workload generated by this real, even if unintentional, consequence of a ruthless focus at work. The example is brutal but too often true: what seemed good for business proved detrimental to the families implicated by it, usually by no choice of their own.

Insofar as their focus is invariably bound up with a proclivity for perfectionism, here is how Italian soccer manager Carlo Ancelotti describes one of the game's most successful coaches: "He [Fabio Capello] was very serious, meticulous and I don't think there is anybody better than him at reading a game. On a human level, well, that's a different story. He didn't have a dialogue with us, he just told us what to do. And, unsurprisingly, he fell out with many players. For example, I remember Ruud Gullit [voted World Soccer Player of the Year in 1987 and 1989] pinning him up against the wall. The rest of us intervened to break it up, even though, secretly, I think many players were cheering for Ruud."[5]

Within the world of commerce, few better examples exist than the late Steve Jobs. Adored around the world for the elegance and user-friendliness of his designs, Jobs was many things, including selfish, rude, aggressive, paranoid, lachrymose, and unpredictable, at least to those who worked with him.[6] But it is his relentless perfectionism (such as making sure the magnetic laptop charger made just the right sort of click) that we adore him for. As Wired.com's news editor, Leander Kahney, wrote before Jobs's premature death:

> Apple creates must-have products the old-fashioned way: by locking the doors and sweating and bleeding until something emerges perfectly formed . . . Jobs is a notorious micromanager. No product escapes Cupertino without meeting Jobs' exacting standards, which are said to cover such esoteric details as the number of screws on the bottom of a laptop and the curve of a monitor's corners . . . At most companies, the red-faced, tyrannical boss is an outdated archetype, a caricature from the life of Dagwood. Not at Apple. Whereas the rest of the tech industry may motivate employees with carrots, Jobs is known as an inveterate stick man. Even the most favored employee could find themselves on the receiving end of a tirade. Insiders have a term for it: the "hero-shithead roller coaster." Jeffrey Bewkes, CEO of Time Warner, found him unvarnished and prone to using colorful language.[7] Says Edward Eigerman, a former Apple engineer, "More than anywhere else I've worked before or since, there's a lot of concern about being fired." . . . A Silicon Valley insider once [said] he had seen Jobs demean many people and make some of them cry. But, the insider added, "He was almost always right."[8]

Couldn't work with him. Wouldn't want a world without him. But do perfectionism, paranoia, tenacity, and self-confidence really make individuals great as well as difficult to manage in a team? Let's explore each of these in turn.

Perfectionism

While it may help raise team performance, the desire to identify scope for improvement can also contribute to a joyless, soul-destroying environment. This is particularly true when perfectionism is triggered by worries about getting it wrong, instead of the desire to make sure every next thing is better than the one before it. The difference is subtle but important. Recent research in psychology suggests that the latter is generally associated with positive experience, whereas the mistake-avoidance variety is associated with anxiety and, paradoxically but importantly, suboptimal performance. Unsurprisingly perhaps, the two are highly correlated, meaning that most of those people who aim for perfection also tend to worry a great deal about making mistakes, even if the latter tends to hamper performance and renders the overall experience much less enjoyable.[9] It creates fatigue and resistance. For that reason, sports psychologists will often spend considerable time helping athletes reframe their ambitions in terms of realizing success as opposed to avoiding failure.

Perfectionism risks creating not just an excessively critical environment but one that, perversely, places a premium on cynicism. Cynicism is often perceived as indicative of smarts and cunning, even if it is rarely helpful. Harvard Business School professor Teresa Amabile makes that point forcefully, having studied cynicism's perceived relation to intelligence. In a clever experiment, she asked people to evaluate a set of carefully crafted book reviews. When her subjects were asked to gauge the reviews, they consistently thought the writers of nasty, acerbic book reviews were more intelligent and also more competent than those who conveyed essentially the same message but in kinder ways.[10] It is one of the curiosities of team life in some societies that we find the contemptuous also the more capable, even if useless for all practical purposes.

Paranoia

The smartest of team members can be surprisingly intuitive when making choices, presumably as a result of having been right so often in the past. As with perfectionism, this is a generalization and, as with any generalization, there are plenty of exceptions. In the workplace, high performers are often keenly aware of their worth to the team but also to the market for talent and might expect instant access to resources and the executive suite.[11] To combine intelligence with the sort of deep-seated insecurities that fuel high performance, particularly within a highly competitive milieu, can breed paranoia.

In his *Playboy* essay on the American chess player Bobby Fischer, for example, Brad Darrach describes his prodigy's media profile as "a sort of paranoid monomaniac who was terrified of girls and Russian spies but worshipped money and Spiro Agnew . . . a high school dropout with a genetic kink who combined the general culture of a hard-rock deejay with a genius for spatial thinking that had made him quite possibly the greatest chess player of all time," even if he drove his support team insane.[12] Darrach's own sketch of Fischer is refreshingly forthright: "He considered himself a superstar, the strongest chess player in the world, and when it came to money, he wanted what superstars like Joe Frazer and Muhammad Ali are offered."[13]

Intel's Andy Grove's autobiography likewise leaves little to the imagination. Success, he thought, breeds complacency, and complacency failure. As the title of his book suggests, only the paranoid survive.

Tenacity

However inspiring the tenacity of baseball's Pete Reiser, his behavior risked jeopardizing the team. Having been told by his physician that he would have to sit out the remainder of the season (having once again hit the wall in attempting a catch), Reiser ripped off his bandages, snuck out of the hospital, took a train to Pittsburgh, and went to the ballpark. Upon arrival, he was told to suit up, not to play but because "it'll give 'em that little spark they need." In the fourteenth inning, however, the team had run out of pinch hitters. Reiser walked up to the bat rack, pulled out his bat, walked up to the plate, and hit a line drive over the second baseman's head—a hit that was good for three bases. With two runs scored, Reiser rounded first base and collapsed. He woke up in the hospital. He continued to play throughout the season, even if dizzy most of the time and unable to see fly balls, which might well have cost them the pennant that year.[14] Less dramatically perhaps, college basketball players, oarsmen, or gymnasts can put the health of their team members at risk by hiding illnesses for fear of deselection—something coaches are well aware of and eager to avoid.

High performers' ambition and intensity occasionally mean they can be explosive in how they deal with those around them. Having won an impressive four Premier League titles in five years with Manchester United, soccer player Eric Cantona's outbursts were as legendary as his contributions, and targeted not just at fellow teammates but at fans, too. Very few managers were willing to deal with his headstrong character.[15] Thus, in a match against London-based soccer club Crystal Palace in early 1995, Cantona was given a red card (a penalty card ejecting him) and sent off after a punishing kick on Palace defender Richard Shaw in response to Shaw pulling his shirt. As he walked toward the tunnel, he launched a kung-fu–style kick at one of Crystal Palace's taunting fans, followed by several punches. He was duly tried and found guilty of bringing "the beautiful game" in disrepute, fined, and banned for eight months. Cantona had snapped, unable to explain his own behavior: "When the hooligan called me 'a French son of a bitch' . . . I had heard it 50 billion times before. However, on that day I did not react as I used to. Why? I never found any answer to that."[16]

Self-Confidence

Despite often deep-seated insecurities, high performers are prone to overestimate the extent to which they are unique and contribute to team performance. These well-documented human traits are exacerbated in many of them. So, for example, most high school students see themselves as above average in intelligence; most business managers see themselves as more competent than average; 90 percent of motorists think themselves safer than average drivers, whereas 94 percent of university professors think themselves better than average teachers. And paradoxically, the bias of seeing ourselves as better than average causes us to see ourselves as less biased than average, too. As psychologist Daniel Gilbert points out, the tendency is not merely for us to see ourselves as more competent but as different from others, too.[17] For example, while people may see themselves as more generous than average, they also tend to see themselves as more selfish than average.

In *What Sport Tells Us About Life*, English cricketer Ed Smith credits this unusually high level of self-assurance for one of sport's more
curious incidents: Zinédine Zidane's head-butting of Italy's Marco
Materazzi in the 2006 World Cup final. It was, in many ways, Europe's
equivalent of Mike Tyson sinking his teeth deep into Evander Holy-
field's right ear. Materazzi fell to the ground. French soccer prodigy Zidane was given the red card and dismissed from the field in
what should have been the swan song of a brilliant career. Everything about the event was bizarre. Zidane had already announced
he would retire after the tournament, and whatever happened, he
would be remembered as one of soccer's greatest players. As Smith
writes: "It was almost as if a great Shakespearean actor, playing King
Lear at the National Theatre for the last time, interrupted his final
soliloquy by punching the dead Cordelia and then announcing his
life-long hatred for producers, directors and—especially—the paying
public. We all like a gracious exit. However, Zidane left us scratching
our heads."[18] Unlike Tyson, Zidane never once apologized for his act
of madness. Nor did he say much about what triggered his reaction
except that it was an "insult to his family" made by Materazzi in the
heat of the game.

In a twist to this popular explanation for his fury, Smith claims
instead that Zidane acted in sheer frustration because the game had
not played out as destined. Any brilliant athlete, thinks Smith, is
convinced of greatness; the greater the athlete, the stronger the conviction. It can turn locker rooms into vipers' nests of egos, cliques,
and fragile psyches.[19] Zidane understood that it was he who was to
turn around France's fortunes in the final few minutes of the tournament, as indeed he had done before on several occasions. And so, in
the 104th minute of the match, Zidane met a perfectly placed cross
on his forehead, his header aiming for the top of the goal. Things
were going as scripted: Zidane had already played and won a World
Cup final and European Championship, having scored twice in each
one, and this final, his third, was to be a replica of those two. His second goal would be France's salvation. What better moment to retire
from the game he loved? Alas, Italy's goalkeeper made a superb save.
Zidane's facial expression was one of unbelief: he had been denied

what was rightfully his. As Smith reckons, the greater an athlete's self-belief, the greater the fall when this is punctured. So, insulted and disillusioned, Zidane blew it all.

That too much self-confidence risks reducing a team to less than the sum of its individual parts is also evident in American football. As former San Francisco 49ers Head Coach Bill Walsh explains:

> There is another side [to ego] that can wreck a team or an orga-
> nization. That is being distracted by your own importance. It can
> come from your insecurity in working with others. It can be the
> need to draw attention to yourself in the public arena. It can be a
> feeling that others are a threat to your own territory. These are all
> negative manifestations of ego, and if you are not alert to them,
> you get diverted and your work becomes diffused. Ego in these
> cases makes people insensitive to how they work with others and
> ends up interfering with the real goal of any group efforts.[20]

What can amount to self-delusion is hardly confined to sports. British men, for example are, on the whole, overly optimistic as to their waist sizes. A recent study points out that the average man thinks he measures 35.8 inches around the waist even if the average waist size is closer to 38 inches. This would be amusing were it not for the fact that any waist larger than 37 inches in circumference correlates with heart disease, diabetes, and cancer.[21]

Cheerier (though no less alarming) is a study reported in a March 1997 issue of *U.S. News & World Report*. One thousand Americans were given a list of names of well-known individuals, including Bill and Hilary Clinton, O.J. Simpson, Princess Diana, Oprah Winfrey, Mother Teresa, Michael Jordan, Al Gore, Pat Robertson, Newt Gingrich, Dennis Rodman, and Colin Powell. They were subsequently asked, for each of these, whether those on the list could be certain of a place in heaven. Unsurprisingly perhaps, Mother Teresa topped the list at 79 percent, followed closely by Oprah Winfrey in second place. Mr. Simpson came last at 19 percent.[22] The follow-up question was no less intriguing. What did these one thousand respondents think would happen to them after death? No less than

87 percent of them were absolutely confident of a place in heaven, effectively beating Mother Teresa to the front of the line.

Closer to our field are responses to two questions asked of 1,800 senior managers.[23] Here's the first: "On a scale of 1 to 5 (5 being 'very confident,' 1 being 'not at all confident'), how confident are you in your own ability to make good choices?" Reassuringly, 83 percent of respondents said they were either "confident" or "very confident" of their ability to make good choices when it came to their professional lives. The second question, as usual, proved the more insightful: "How confident are you in the ability of those you work with most closely to also make good choices?" Most people anticipate that the 83 percent of self-reported self-confidence will take a beating. Few are, however, prepared for the extent of the nosedive: of the 1,800 managers surveyed, only 27 percent were either "confident" or "very confident" of the ability of their colleagues to also make good choices.

Now, of course, there is something quite ironic about this: if you happen to have been involved in hiring these colleagues, there is clearly something amiss with your ability to make good choices. That said, these survey results illustrate not just our tendency to overestimate our own abilities but, worryingly, our underestimating the abilities of others. What few seem to realize is that those we work with are often far more perceptive of being underestimated than we think they are. And, as a general rule, people resent being underestimated, particularly by those they work with every day.

It is this inferior, and often poorly grounded, assessment of the skills of others compared to one's own that can be the scourge of professional service firms. Steve Hollis, a senior partner with KPMG, has worked with a multiplicity of teams in Europe and globally. His assessment is refreshingly candid: "All too often our clients question why, with our unparalleled knowledge of their business, we can't do more to help them. All too often I find the root cause is the natural instinct to protect what we have and not risk introducing a colleague who may put all of our achievements at risk."[24]

Our relative lack of ability in many areas of life also makes us less likely to recognize when we are incompetent.[25] A nice, even if rather unusual, example of this is the story of McArthur Wheeler who, in 1995, robbed two Pittsburgh banks in broad daylight. He had made no visible attempt at disguise. Aided by surveillance tapes, the police were able to arrest him later that night. When, as part of the procedure, they showed Wheeler the video footage of him carrying out the crime, he acted in disbelief, claiming he "wore the juice." Apparently, Wheeler had been under the impression that rubbing lemon juice on one's face made one undetectable to security cameras. As the *Pittsburgh Post-Gazette* put it at the time, Wheeler might have had larceny in his heart but little in his head.[26]

But Perform They Do

Of course, not all this is bad news. If individuals didn't share at least some of these characteristics, it is unlikely that any of them (with the exception of Mr. Wheeler) would have achieved quite as much as they did. As professional service firms know particularly well, sometimes those most difficult to get along with can also be the greatest rainmakers.

A telling counterpart to soccer's Cantona and Zidane is Morgan Stanley capital markets division's Rob Parson, the protagonist of a popular Harvard Business School case study. Performance appraisals for Parson suggested his colleagues found him to be sharp-tongued, impatient, and generally just difficult to work with. Although he was an unlikely candidate, Morgan Stanley had snapped him up after a successful stint with three major investment houses. As Parson himself had already suspected, the fit was far from perfect. While generating vast revenues for the firm, he had never quite fit the consensus-building, team-based culture of Morgan Stanley. As Paul Nasr, who recruited him, despairingly summarized: "He has created a hostile environment around him. The syndicate guys are not happy with him basically questioning their prices. The traders are not happy with him questioning their knowledge of the markets.

And he always thinks he has the right answer, and the majority of the times he does have the right answer, but every time he comes up with the right answer on his own, a lot of people feel undermined."[27] Despite his rough edges, Parson was valued for his ability to cross-sell and to make introductions and share information, and for the energy he brought to bear on his work.[28]

Managing the Good with the Bad

Why is it that Cantona, Zidane, and Parson are so good and yet so bad? The answer may lie in some specific traits that, while desirable, risk derailing teams. By implication, team leadership is as much about mitigating the risks of these traits as it is about exploiting their potential. So, for example, self-belief can lead people to be more decisive, yet they risk being seen as domineering. An added dose of intelligence is useful in allowing someone to quickly grasp the complexity of the issue at hand, yet risks dismissing the contributions of others. High performers are unusually restless. As a recent survey of one hundred high achievers suggests, their single most common trait was discontent.[29] Restlessness fuels productivity. But it can cause people to be impatient with those around them as well. That they have high expectations leads them to set and achieve ambitious goals, yet can make those around them feel unable to fully satisfy expectations.

People who are disciplined are useful insofar as they foster efficiency and productivity, yet they risk being accused of entertaining unrealistic expectations. Their charisma can help bring out the best in others, yet they risk being manipulative in luring others into particular ways of doing things. They are determined to win and hate getting the short end of the stick, meaning they often end up getting what they want. And yet because everything becomes a competition of sorts, their behavior can be threatening to their peers. They are often tenacious but can drive others to exhaustion. Unafraid of change, and lured by the promise of newness, they risk taking action before the requisite buy-in of colleagues. Their farsightedness is valuable in discovering whatever gaps there are between today and tomorrow but often at the expense of focusing on what needs to be done now. The strength of their convictions makes them believable but can cause them to become defensive when challenged.[30]

Talent Q Group has compiled assessment data from over fourteen thousand individuals adding further traits that risk derailing teams when under pressure: hypersensitivity, as a result of being overly anxious and often surprisingly fragile emotionally; isolation, particularly when also being poor communicators; iconoclasm, or being willing to break with convention but, in doing so, being insensitive to those around them; attention-seeking behavior, making them prone to exaggerating; and, as in Steve Jobs's case, a tendency to micromanage the affairs of others.[31]

Thus, high performers oscillate between healthy and irritating behaviors. As Work Ethic's Kate Ludeman and Eddie Erlandson write, "their magnetic leadership commands respect, but their aggressive tactics create resistance, resentment and revenge. They are celebrated for their achievements but loathed for the carnage they leave in their wake. People stand in awe of their competence and can-do energy, but they often hate reporting to them or teaming with them."[32]

Many employees nowadays spend ten or more hours a month complaining about their bosses (or listening to similar complaints by others), while around one-third spent twenty hours doing so, and occasionally far more.[33] Internet blogs are a rich source of such complaints. Take this one for example:

[My boss] pays me $20 hr to basically take messages on little scraps of paper (I'm not allowed to have a message book) and write up invoices, etc that he dictates word for word and totals in Excel, so he can verify how Quickbook calculates! But I am called the office manager and referred to as "her." He insults the crew and customers all day, every day. He's taken a successful company and has ruined it by changing everything that worked to "his way" . . . he's totally inconsistent . . . messes up everything, wastes everyone's time . . . This is the worse case of a clueless, control freak narcissist I have ever encountered and I'm 58 years old. He plays on the computer all day, crunches Fritos (loudly) burps, sneezes, sighs constantly . . . spits tobacco in the garbage cans & bathroom sink. I have never heard him say excuse me. Rather, the bigger the burp, the prouder he is.[34]

Robert Sutton's *The No Asshole Rule* pulls no punches either. His arsenal includes studies of U.S. nurses as recipients of verbal abuse from physicians. One of these, conducted in 1997 and written up in the *Journal of Professional Nursing*, found that 90 percent of the 130 nurses surveyed reported being victims of verbal abuse over the previous twelve months. A similar study published in *Orthopaedic Nursing* surveyed 461 nurses of whom 91 percent reported similar complaints, but within a single month.[35]

The Leadership Challenge

So it seems we cannot have our cake and eat it too. Or can we? A first step is surely to acknowledge the risks entailed in our own behavior, and to set clear limits as to what behavior is and isn't acceptable on the team. The risk of an individual derailing a team can be mitigated by helping him to realize that his behavior may ultimately thwart his own potential.

Duke University's legendary coach Mike Krzyzewski holds "irritant meetings," challenging his staff and players to think of as many irritants as possible and—in the spirit of "let's not let Duke beat Duke"—to have them out in the open for discussion. The complaints can be something as simple as bad food or accommodation, tardiness of one or more team members, inflammatory language, personal hygiene, sloppiness, lack of engagement or perceived lack of commitment, or even someone not speaking out when they should.[36]

Like the proverbial dead fish under the boardroom table, if you leave it there long enough, it will start to stink. Anecdotal observations suggest that conversations and meetings like Krzyzewski's can be helped by relying on "hard facts" insofar as objective data feeds the analytical part of the brain.[37] By their very nature, high performers are uncomfortable exposing their insecurities. To substantiate this, we need look no further than the proliferation of "corporate coaches" who are engaged, often confidentially, to help senior executives come to terms with their inner demons. Sports teams have long done likewise by retaining the services of sports psychologists.

Team Bonding

Aware of the risk of derailment, those tasked with leading teams have often resorted to "away days," retreats, or corporate team-bonding exercises. Chances are that you have already thrown considerable resources at team-building exercises: trivia nights, military-style boot camps, treasure hunts, wine tastings, traversing hot coals, building towers from bits of trash, or tracking down fugitives, their variety limited only to the human imagination and corporate budget. Their effects are often short-lived, and their consequences occasionally costly.

Athletes too seek out team-building events, even though the events can polarize as much as bond. Former Australian cricketer, Shane Warne, recommends against them, worried about the injuries they might cause. "I am from the old school," he says. "If you want to gel everyone together, lock them up in a pub and do not let anyone come in. Sometimes after a long summer of cricket, players are better off spending time away from each other so they can recharge the batteries. Not a boot camp."[38] Steve Waugh, his former captain, disagrees: "To me, 'bonding' is an overrated term normally linked to reminiscing about past escapades with a truckload of grog on board. I've had my fair share of these nights, and while they can create a few laughs and a better understanding of each other, the experience is shallow and soon forgotten.[39]

To make sure they are not shallow, the events occasionally include periods of collective reflection, such as the Australian cricket team's trip to Gallipoli and the Somme, or the England cricket team's visit to Flanders Field and Dachau.[40] England captain Andrew Strauss's description of the bonding experience as a "tough but rewarding five days" took on more meaning when the England and Wales Cricket Board publicly confirmed that one of the team, James Anderson, had suffered a cracked rib during a boxing match against another teammate.[41] Then again, the England team did go on to win the 2010 Ashes, arguably cricket's most famous prize.

Occasionally, the exercises get bizarre. Take, for example, Alarm One Inc.'s decision to pit sales teams against each other in an exercise where the winners would poke fun at the losers, throwing pies at them, feeding them baby food, making them wear diapers, and swatting their buttocks. One "losing" employee, Janet Orlando, subsequently sued the California home security company for having spanked her with a competitor's yard sign; the company ended up paying $1.7 million for the privilege. Or consider the example of Chad Hudgens, until recently employed by Utah-based motivational coaching firm Prosper Inc. After volunteering for a new but undisclosed team-building exercise, he was taken outside and pinned to the ground by colleagues before his enterprising boss proceeded to pour water all over his face, telling Hudgens's team members all the while that he wanted them to work as hard on sales as Hudgens did at breathing. Needless to say, Hudgens has since sued his employer.

As a correspondent for the *Times of London* writes: "Nobody worries about team spirit on the factory floor. You never see teams of assembly-line workers scaling rock faces in East London . . . Only the pretentious and the terminally short of ideas feel that there is anything to be gained from being strapped into a canoe with some halfwit from marketing, and having an ex-commando bark instructions at you for a day."[42]

More auspicious perhaps is a recent study by three University of California–Berkeley psychologists on the effect of touch on team performance. By coding the touch behavior of 294 players from all thirty National Basketball Association (NBA) teams during the 2008–2009 season, they discovered that frequent touching early on predicted greater performance for teams as well as individuals later in the season. When controlling for player status, preseason expectations, and early season performance, their hypothesis that touch predicted improved performance still held. Intuitively this makes sense. By touching—using high fives, chest bumps, leaping shoulder bumps, chest punches, head slaps, head grabs, low fives, high tens, full hugs, half hugs, and team huddles—we communicate cooperation, and help lay to rest the anxieties experienced by others in communicating affect, reassurance, and trust.[43] The practicalities of generalizing these findings to the bank, law firm, or boardroom, however, are less clear-cut.

The "Stephens Question"

A more promising antidote is that of galvanizing teams around a credible cause. And here is where sporting teams often have it over their corporate cousins. The Cambridge University Boat Club (CUBC) has always had a single objective. Founded in 1828 by two students, one from the University of Oxford, the other from Cambridge University, the club's goal remains that of beating Oxford in the annual Boat Race. This race is still rowed "at or near London, each in an eight-oared boat during the Easter vacation" in full view of the public. As the second-oldest varsity match in the world (cricket predates it by one year), it attracts a quarter of a million people on the banks of the River Thames and a television audience of an estimated 120 million around the world.

The question as to why this student race should hold such universal appeal is itself interesting: Is it because it involves two of the world's grandest institutions of learning, the intellectual homes of Lewis Carroll, John Maynard Keynes, W. H. Auden, Stephen Hawking, and C. S. Lewis? Is it the secrecy surrounding crew selection and race preparation? Is it because rowing has mostly remained an amateur sport, meaning that either university crew will often field Olympians and world champions? Or is it because it has always been a thing of sharp contrasts: passionately amateur and yet holding to professional standards, a world of mutual respect yet intense rivalry, where it's all about taking part but where the pain of losing is intolerable?

Perhaps it is the all-or-nothing character of the race, as four-time Olympic gold medalist Matthew Pinsent explains: "You must have huge courage to put yourself through all that is required to earn your seat, and row the race. There's something very alluring about putting yourself through all that, in order to row a race where the prize is a small medal in a little box. The pain is so worthwhile, but the penalties for losing are really high too. In other walks of life there is much to achieve even if you don't win, whereas in the Boat Race it's all or nothing."[44]

Few workplaces can compete with as compelling and simple a purpose. It allows the CUBC to strip complex, often highly emotive decisions to their bare bones. They call it the "Stephens Question," so-named after an influential former club manager, Roger Stephens: "Will doing this make the boat faster?" The answer is ultimately a straightforward yes or no. Notwithstanding the fact that most workplaces are vastly more complex in their pursuit of multiple objectives, would it help to try and distill, at the level of the team, an equivalent of a Stephens Question? The predictable, "Will this increase shareholder value?" may be the correct test as far as senior management or corporate boards are concerned but it is unlikely to inspire. The real question is what will.

Reprinted from *There Is an I in Team* by Mark de Rond
(Boston: Harvard Business Review Press, 2012).

Notes

1. See L. J. Wertheim and T. Moskowitz, *Scorecasting: The Hidden Influences Behind How Sports Are Played and Games Are Won* (New York: Crown Archetype, 2011). As Wertheim and Moskowitz note, it is a rarity for a basketball team without superstars to make it to the playoffs, let alone finals. When compiling a register of the top eight basketball players, using such criteria as first-team all-stars, top-five MVP vote-getters, or even salaries, they noticed at least one of these featured in all but one NBA finals series for the last three decades.

2. See D. Whitaker, *The Spirit of Teams* (Marlborough, UK: The Crowood Press, 1999), 12.

3. See W. C. Heinz's essay, "The Rocky Road of Pistol Pete," in *The Best American Sports Writing of the Century*, ed. David Halberstam (New York: Houghton Mifflin, 1999), 289–303, quote, 236–237.

4. Ibid.

5. See Carlo Ancelotti, *The Beautiful Games of an Ordinary Genius* (New York: Rizzolo International Publications, 2010). This quote from a prepublication online review.

6. See Walter Isaacson, "Rages, Tears and Hugs: No One Was Immune to Steve's Folly," *The Sunday Times*, 30 October 2011, 2.

7. See John Arlidge, "A World in Thrall to the iTyrant," *The Sunday Times*, October 9, 2011, 2–3.

8. See http://www.wired.com/techbiz/it/magazine/16-04/bz_apple.

9. See, for example, Joachim Stoeber, "Striving to Achieve Perfection: How Perfectionism Affects Aspirations, Emotions, and Results in Achievement Situations," working paper, The Social Life of Achievement workshop, Department of Social Anthropology, Cambridge University, September 30, 2010.

10. Teresa Amabile, "Brilliant But Cruel," *Journal of Experimental Social Psychology* 19, no. 2 (March 1983): 146–156.

11. See Rob Goffee and Gareth Jones, "Why Should Anyone Be Led by You?" *Harvard Business Review*, September 2000.

12. See Brad Darrach's wonderful essay, "The Day Bobby Blew It," in *The Best American Sports Writing of the Century*, ed. David Halberstam (New York: Houghton Mifflin, 1999), 90–128, quote, 92.

13. Ibid., 99.

14. Ibid., 243.

15. For a more elaborate description, see David Bolchover and Chris Brady, *The 90-Minute Manager* (London: Financial Times Management), 198. As the authors explain, his manager at Leeds United, Howard Wilkinson, believed that Cantona was not a team-player, omitting him from many games, and ultimately selling him to Manchester United.

16. From Jean-Philippe Leclaire and Jérôme Cazadieu, "King Eric: Ten Years On," *The Sunday Times*, May 13, 2007.

17. For a more elaborate discussion of these traits, see Daniel Gilbert, *Stumbling on Happiness* (New York: Alfred Knopf, 2006), 252–255.

18. Ed Smith, *What Sport Tells Us About Life* (London: Penguin, 2008), 29.

19. This is how Steve James described the 2010 English cricket team in *The Telegraph*, September 28, 2010, as it prepared to face Australia in the Ashes, in "The Ashes 2010: England's Boot-Camp Experience Is Just Not Cricket."

20. See Richard Rapaport's interview with Bill Walsh, "To Build a Winning Team: An Interview with Head Coach Bill Walsh," *Harvard Business Review*, January 1993. Norman Mailer's 1971 feature on Muhammad Ali is telling in this respect, too. As he wrote in *Life*: "Muhammad Ali begins with the most unsettling ego of all. Having commanded the stage, he never pretends to step back and relinquish his place to other actors—like a six-foot parrot, he keeps screaming at you that he is the center of the stage. 'Come here and get me, fool,' he says. 'You can't, 'cause you don't know who I am. You don't know *where* I am. I'm human intelligence and you don't even know if I'm good or evil.' This has been his essential message to America all these years. It is intolerable to our American mentality that the figure who is probably most prominent to us after the president is simply not comprehensible, for he could be a demon or a saint." See Norman Mailer, "Ego," in *The Best American Sports Writing of the Century*, ed. David Halberstam (New York: Houghton Mifflin, 1999), 713–737, quote, 713.

21. See *The Week* (UK ed.), October 15, 2011, 23.

22. As published in *U.S. News & World Report*, March 23, 1997, based on a poll of 1,000 Americans conducted by Market Facts. The full results are as follows: Mother Teresa (79%), Oprah Winfrey (66%), Michael Jordan (65%), Colin Powell (61%), Princess Diana (60%), Al Gore (55%), Hilary Clinton (55%), Bill Clinton (52%), Pat Robertson (47%), Newt Gingrich (40%), Dennis Rodman (28%), O.J. Simpson (19%). Survey instruments like this are blunt instruments and may need to be taken with a pinch of salt. For example, much depends on the religious views of the respondent, and the criteria he or she thinks apply when making judgments on who is, and isn't, heaven-bound. Also, the list is a predominantly Christian one. One can be forgiven for concluding that it reads much like a popularity contest.

23. The survey results are described in D. Marcum and S. Smith, *Egonomics: What Makes Our Ego Our Greatest Asset (Or Most Expensive Liability)* (New York: Simon & Schuster, 2008).

24. Steve Hollis, interview with author, May 9, 2011.

25. See, for example, Justin Kruger and David Dunning, "Unskilled and Unaware of It: How Difficulties in Recognizing One's Own Incompetence Lead to Inflated Self-assessments," *Journal of Personality and Social Psychology* 77, no. 6 (1999): 1121–1134.

26. M. A. Fuocco, "Trial and Error: They Had Larceny in Their Hearts, but Little in Their Heads," *Pittsburgh Post-Gazette*, D1, as quoted in ibid. My favorite example of stupidity in crime is Kasey G. Kazee's attempt to rob a liquor store in Ashland, Kentucky, in August 2007. In an attempt to disguise himself, he had wrapped his head in duct tape. Luckily for Kasey, it was a hot day and his sweat prevented the tape from ripping off his eyebrows when the police tore off the duct tape in an attempt to identify him.

27. From M. Diane Burton, "Rob Parson at Morgan Stanley (A)," Case 498-054 (Boston: Harvard Business School, 1998), Nasr is quoted on p. 5 of the case.

28. On matters of promotion, one of the 2010 Ig Nobel Prizes was awarded to a piece of research that, controversially, shows, by means of agent-based simulations, that not only is the Peter Principle (implying that people are promoted until they reach their maximum level of incompetence) unavoidable, but also it yields in turn a significant reduction of the global efficiency of the organization. Within a game-theory-like approach, the three authors (Alessandro Pluchino and his team at the Universitá di Catania) explored different promotion strategies and found that in order to avoid such an effect, the best ways for improving the efficiency of a given organization are either to promote an agent each time at random or to promote randomly the best and the worst members in terms of competence. So in mathematical terms, at least, it makes the most sense to promote incompetence. Sometimes.

29. Maulana wahlduddln Khan, "Depression as Blessing," *The Times of India*, May 24, 2011.

30. For more details on these traits (their benefits and risks), see Kate Ludeman and Eddie Erlandson, *Alpha Male Syndrome* (Boston: Harvard Business School Press, 2006), 12, 78.

31. Dr. Alan Bourne and Richard A. Mackinnon, "Personality and Leadership Derailment," white paper, Talent Q, info@talentq.co.uk.

32. See Ludeman and Erlandson, *Alpha Male Syndrome*, 8–9. While good estimates are hard to come by, the authors suspect 75% of top executives to be "alphas." One could argue, of course, that this high estimate reflects a typically "Western" perspective, with alpha traits being expressed differently (if at all) in societies that place a premium on collaborative problem solving, modesty, humility, and equality. And while Ludeman and Erlandson focus on alpha males, they make it clear that many of the traits attributed to these males are true of alpha females too (even if females tend to express them differently).

33. See badbossology.com for some interesting data on "bad" bosses. The survey was sponsored by Development Dimensions International.

34. The entry can be found at http://www.badbossology.com/i128879.

35. See Robert Sutton, *The No Asshole Rule* (London: Sphere, 2007), 19.

36. See S. B. Sitkin and J. R. Hackman, "Developing Team Leadership: An Interview with Coach Mike Krzyzewski," *Academy of Management Learning & Education* 10, no. 3 (2011): 494–501.

37. Alpha traits are not confined to men, of course. As Ludeman and Erlandson write, there are few differences between genders when it comes to competitiveness and drive. There do seem to be differences in the way these traits are expressed. For example, men scored higher than women on impatience and the difficulty of controlling their anger, whereas women are usually less overt. Women are emotionally more intelligent and will often prefer to seek consensus. Their ability to empathize and be sensitive to the feelings of others can pay dividends but could be ineffective when dealing with those who need a more direct approach. And conflict avoidance can suppress internal competition, or drive it underground, and clear the air by exchanging strongly held points of view. So it seems one cannot have one's cake and eat it too.

38. Steve James, "The Ashes 2010: England's Boot Camp Experience Is Just Not Cricket," *The Telegraph*, October 28, 2010.

39. Ibid.

40. Nick Hoult, "The Ashes 2010: England's Secret Bonding Trip Was Beneficial, Says Andrew Strauss," *The Telegraph*, October 28, 2010.

41. Andy Wilson, "England's 'Boot Camp' Called into Question After James Anderson Injury," *Guardian*, October 15, 2010.

42. Martin Samuels in *The Times* as reprinted in *The Week*, November 10, 2007, 10.

43. See Michael W. Kraus, Cassy Huang, and Dacher Keltner, "Tactile Communication, Cooperation, and Performance: An Ethological Study of the NBA," working paper, University of California–Berkeley, 2010.

44. Julian Andrews, *What It Takes to Earn Your Place* (London: Third Millennium Publishing, Ltd., 2004), 12.

An Interview with Andre Agassi

Andre Agassi *started his tennis career "in diapers" and ended it at age 36, having won eight Grand Slam titles. Married (to fellow champion Steffi Graf) with two kids, he now oversees a foundation and a charter school in Las Vegas where accountability is the mantra. No courts on campus, though. "The idea that I succeed at your demise doesn't fit the culture," he explains.* **Interviewed by Alison Beard**

HBR: *In your autobiography you say that you hate tennis. Why did you play for so long?*

Agassi: At first it was a lack of alternatives. As a child, I knew nothing but success would be accepted. Or, if I didn't succeed, it would take a toll on our family. So I put my head down and did the best I could. Then, being sent away to an academy at 13, the only way out was to succeed. You don't know what else you're going to do, and fear is one hell of a motivator. After that it becomes your life, and you have some success, and the world tells you that you should be thrilled. So you keep living the Groundhog Day, the hamster wheel. I thought that getting to number one was going to be the moment I made sense of my life. But it left me a little empty, and I spiraled down until something had to change.

Then you executed a legendary comeback. You'd had enough success, and earned enough money, to retire happily to Las Vegas at that point, so why keep at it?

It wouldn't have been retiring happily. It would have been quitting miserably. I was at a critical point where if I made one more misstep, I wouldn't get a chance to be on the court again, and the climb back would have been truly impossible. So I made a commitment to take ownership of my life. I started to get more connected, and then I just kept going with tangible daily goals. It wasn't about a destination. Getting back to number one was something I was pretty convinced I'd never achieve. But that journey from rock bottom to the summit a second time was a great accomplishment for me. Without it I don't know if I would believe in myself as much as I do when I face other challenges now.

You had epic match comebacks too. How did you develop that resilience?

It's about recognizing that regardless of what the score is, the most important point is that next point. If you can get yourself into that state of mind, you just are who you are. People give you more credit for coming back than they do for blowing somebody out, but both require the same skill set. After a blowout, nobody says, "Wow, how strong and focused you are." But you really are.

What distinguishes the best tennis players from the rest?

You need an arsenal of tools that give you an advantage over the field. It helps to have two or three possible game plans, especially in those matches when you've got to figure out a way to win. When you get on the court, it's all about what you've done leading up to that day—whether you've done your homework, prepared right, trained hard enough, put enough fluids in your body. You have to do all those things a little bit better than the person you'll be measured against. It's really perfectionism.

Are there skills that your wife had as a competitor that you wish you'd had?

She had an athleticism over her peers that was quite a luxury. When she was in full form, she was just a horse that wasn't going to be caught. For me, it wasn't like that. I couldn't just steamroll past people because I was such an athlete or talented in all these different ways. I had a couple of strengths, but I had to out-think everybody and implement my strategies one piece at a time, like a puzzle. That's more exhausting, and you don't get the results as consistently.

How did you learn to manage your emotions when you played?

I don't know that I did. I've seen people use emotion, positive or negative, as a tool, and it works for them. But typically, the more you can remove emotion, the more efficient you'll be. You can be an inch from winning but still miles away if you allow emotion to interfere with the last step. So you have to accept: the weather, heat, rain, stops and starts, the line calls, whatever your opponent is giving you, however tired or injured you are. There are so many things that can distract you from taking care of business. The only thing you can control is your engagement.

How did your rivalries help or hurt you?

A great rival is like a mirror. You have to look at yourself, acknowledge where you fall short, make adjustments, and nurture the areas where you overachieve. There were times my rivals brought out the best in me; there were times they brought out the worst. They probably helped me win things I never would have otherwise; they also cost me titles. I don't know how you quantify what it would have been like without a rival like Pete Sampras. I would have won more. But I think I would have been worse without him.

You completely remade your image over the course of your career. Tell me about that process.

I would challenge any adult to look at their teenaged self and tell me what they recognize. I went through some heavy transitions, discovering and learning myself along the way. But it was all authentic.

How did you approach retirement?

It was one of the hardest things I've ever had to go through emotionally. Think about it: You've done this thing since you were in diapers. You don't remember life without it. It's really the only thing you do. Then one day it comes to an end, and you have no idea what's on the other side because you don't even know yourself without it. It's like planning for death: *Let's see, in the afterlife I want to do this and do that.* It just doesn't compute. I couldn't process how, moving forward, I would never have to do the things I'd always had to do. But you start with what you can control: What will I do today? And then every day was a discovery, and it was a nice feeling. I felt empowered.

At the C2 Montreal conference earlier this year, you said a typical day for you now involves working in the morning but finishing by 2:30 in the afternoon to pick up your kids in the carpool line.

I have the luxury of tweaking the balance now, of never missing a baseball game or a dance competition. If I'm feeling like I need a business outlet, I plan work. But yes, I engage much harder with my kids because they grow up fast. By the time you're qualified for the job, you're unemployed.

What do you regard as your biggest career mistake?

I wish I had taken ownership of the business side of my career years ago instead of trusting certain people. Nobody cares more, or represents you better, than you do yourself.

How do you pick employees and business partners now?

I'm a big fan of people who do more than they say. People who enjoy puffing their chest out and acting as if they're really smart and can handle everything always disappoint you.

Who are the mentors you've learned the most from, on and off the court?

A father's relationship with his son is formative—for better or worse. You learn what you want to be and what you don't. Gil, my trainer, helped me feel worth being cared about, which was a big deal in my world. On the court he pushed me physically in ways that allowed me to get around some inherent liabilities with my body and to get better as I got older. I didn't always train harder—I trained smarter, and that was because of him. Then I would say my wife, who inspires me in a lot of ways. I'm more efficient in everything I do because of how she chooses to be. There are things she clearly cares about and things she doesn't. She just doesn't have energy for stuff that isn't contributing to her engagement. And that clarity is a jewel. I'd throw in Nick Bollettieri. The impact he had on me was both good and bad, personally and professionally, but I don't think I could have achieved as much without having been in his environment. Brad Gilbert was the one to really teach me how to play tennis, how to think for myself from a strategic standpoint when I was out there. Then Darren [Cahill] gave me some of the great years that I never would have had without him—those years when I was old enough to really appreciate everything.

What distinguishes the best coaches from the rest?

Coaching is not what you know. It's what your student learns. And for your student to learn, you have to learn him. The greats spend a lot of time understanding where the player is. The day they stop learning is the day they should stop teaching.

That's a nice segue into your foundation and school. What do you think is wrong with the way kids are educated today, and how are you trying to fix it?

As long as we're making education about the adults and not the children, that's a problem. There are a lot of agendas being pursued at a cost to our kids, and resources are irrelevant if there's no accountability as to how they're used. What I think we really need is a children's union. My own mission is to focus on impact. I'm not one to sit in a boardroom and talk about something. I'd rather roll up my sleeves and get in the trenches. Clark County in Las Vegas is the fifth largest school district in America, and we're 50th as measured by the kids we put into college—so what a great testing laboratory.

What sets your school apart?

One difference is time on task. There are no shortcuts. We have longer school days—eight hours versus six. If you add that up, it's 16 years of education versus 12 for district peers. There's also an emphasis on accountability, which starts with the kids themselves. They know this is a privilege: There are 1,000 kids on the waiting list. So they take ownership. The teachers have annual contracts; there's no business in the world that could succeed if employees who worked for three years got a job for life. The parents are accountable too. They need to acknowledge, accept, and embrace the objectives set for their children. They come in, they volunteer time, they sign off on homework assignments. You have to cover all the bases.

Originally published in October 2015. Reprint R1510K

Why Sports Are a Terrible Metaphor for Business

by Bill Taylor

HERE IN THE UNITED STATES, the Super Bowl is the biggest game in America's biggest sport. The buzz around the game is, as always, about more than football. It's also about business and leadership. Does the Patriots's consistent excellence over the last 15 years offer insights on teamwork that transcend football? Does Bill Belichick's unrivaled record speak to his skills not just as a coach but also as a leader from whom others can learn? Even as high-minded a publication as *The Economist* gets caught up every so often in the connections between sports and business. A few years back, writing about a team that was dominating a different kind of football, the magazine claimed that FC Barcelona, the renowned soccer club, "has provided a distinctive solution to some of the most contentious problems in management theory." Wow!

So the question becomes: What can sports in general, and football in particular, teach us about competition and success, talent and teamwork, value and values? My answer, I'm afraid, is "not very much." Sports, it turns out, are a terrible metaphor for business, and leaders who look to the gridiron or the soccer pitch for ideas about their work will be sorely disappointed.

Here's what's wrong with making analogies between sports and business.

The logic of competition and success is completely different.
What makes football or basketball so exhilarating is that only one team wins at the end of a season. In the case of the Super Bowl, there is one world champion, and 31 NFL teams with crushed dreams and dispirited fans. For one team to win, every other team must lose. The logic of business competition is nothing like this. The most successful companies, those that win big and create the most economic value, worry less about crushing the competition than about delighting and amazing their customers. The very idea of zero-sum competition (for me to win, you must lose) feels like a relic from a long-ago era of business. Virtually every industry has room for plenty of different winners, each of which is great at serving a distinct piece of the market or a certain set of customers.

A few years ago, during the research for our book *Mavericks at Work*, Polly LaBarre and I spent time with Mike McCue, one of the great entrepreneurs in Silicon Valley. Here's how he explained his approach to strategy and success: "Even in the face of massive competition, don't think about the competition. Literally don't think about them. Every time you're in a meeting and you're tempted to talk about a competitor, replace that thought with one about user feedbacks or surveys. Just think about the customer."

The dynamics of talent and teamwork are completely different.
You'd think business organizations would have lots to learn from high-performing sports teams such as the New England Patriots, but there are huge weaknesses in the comparisons, which makes the analogy virtually useless. Most important, "teamwork" in the NFL means teamwork among players whose careers are absurdly short and whose loyalties to any one team only last as long as the duration of their contracts. According to the *Wall Street Journal*, the average length of an NFL career is 2.66 years.

So the job of an NFL coach is to yell, threaten, and otherwise cajole maximum effort from players who have almost no expectation of sticking around for very long. What sane company would take that approach? Organizations that are building for the long term, that hope to attract, grow, and retain the best people in their fields, and that wish to create an environment where great people do their best work year after year have little to learn from the short-term, utterly disposable mentality that defines life in the NFL. Most football teams, to be brutally honest, are a collection of mercenaries ruled by a tyrant. That's not how great business organizations work.

The creation of economic value is completely different.

Even the most ardent sports fans are quick to agree with the idea that sports is a business. And the business of sports, it turns out, may offer even fewer lessons for business leaders than what happens on the field. Unlike most billion-dollar businesses, which are owned by shareholders and governed by a board of directors, nearly every NFL team is owned by a single individual, and they are accountable to virtually no one besides the other billionaire owners. The one notable exception is the Green Bay Packers, which are structured as a nonprofit organization and are run to benefit the community.

NFL owners have reaped vast riches over the last 20 years, negotiating huge television contracts, demanding big subsidies for taxpayers, and devising new ways to profit from the internet. Their hardball tactics have made them very wealthy—but very unpopular with fans. Remember that old expression, "Don't hate the player, hate the game"? Well, NFL fans (and fans of most sports, truth be told) love the players, but hate the owners. Sure, there are plenty of unpopular CEOs out there, but would any publicly traded company put up with a CEO who is as unpopular with its customers (fans) as, say, Chargers owner Alex Spanos is with the residents of San Diego, or as Rams owner Stan Kroenke is with the people of St. Louis?

And don't even get fans started on NFL commissioner Roger Goodell, who may be the single most unpopular executive in all of sports. It's hard to square the unprecedented popularity of football with the universal unpopularity of NFL owners, but that's the business of sports—and another reason why sports are a lousy metaphor for business. It's hard to learn many leadership lessons from an industry whose leaders are burned in effigy or booed at huge public gatherings.

So I hope everyone has a great time watching the Super Bowl. But the idea that what happens on the field (or in the team executives' offices) teaches us anything about what should happen inside other organizations is misguided. It's fun to be a student of the game, but let's not kid ourselves that any lessons we learn from sports apply to our roles as company builders or business leaders.

Originally published in February 2017. Reprint H03FPH

About the Contributors

KAREEM ABDUL-JABBAR is a celebrated former professional basketball player. More recently he has become a successful writer, historian, and filmmaker.

ANDRE AGASSI is a former professional tennis player with eight Grand Slam titles to his name. He now oversees a foundation and a charter school in Las Vegas.

SCOTT D. ANTHONY (@ScottDAnthony) is managing partner of the growth strategy consulting firm Innosight and co-author of the book, *Dual Transformation: How to Reposition Today's Business While Creating the Future* (Harvard Business Review Press, 2017).

MIKHAIL BARYSHNIKOV is a ballet dancer who is a former star of the Kirov Ballet. In 1974 he defected to Canada, then settled in the U.S. at the American Ballet Theatre, where he later became artistic director. He left in 1989 to cofound a modern dance company and take on film, theater, and TV roles. He is now the artistic director of the Baryshnikov Arts Center and, at age 63, still performs.

ALISON BEARD is a senior editor at *Harvard Business Review*.

KATHERINE BELL is the former Editor of HBR.org.

MARK DE ROND is a Cambridge University–based ethnographer.

ANITA ELBERSE is the Lincoln Filene Professor of Business Administration at Harvard Business School and the author of *Blockbusters: Hit-making, Risk-taking, and the Big Business of Entertainment* (Henry Holt, 2013).

SIR ALEX FERGUSON is a famed coach of the Manchester United football team, where he spent 26 seasons, during which time the team won 13 English league titles along with 25 other domestic and international trophies.

JOE GIRARDI is a former manager of the New York Yankees. He was named National League Manager of the Year after his only year with the Florida Marlins in 2006, and he led the Yankees to their 27th World Series win in 2009. He played catcher for five Major League Baseball teams over his 15-year career.

SARAH GREEN CARMICHAEL is a senior editor at *Harvard Business Review*. Follow her on Twitter at @skgreen.

ALEX GREGORY is an Olympic rower and World Champion.

GRAHAM JONES, PHD, has consulted to top performers in business, athletics, and the military for more than 20 years. He was Professor of Elite Performance Psychology at the University of Wales, Bangor. His most recent book is *Thrive On Pressure: Lead and Succeed When Times Get Tough* (McGraw-Hill, 2010). He is currently the Managing Director of Top Performance Consulting Ltd., based in Wokingham in the United Kingdom.

JIM LOEHR, a performance psychologist, has worked with hundreds of professional athletes, including Monica Seles, Dan Jansen, and Mark O'Meara. Loehr is also a cofounder and the CEO of LGE Performance Systems in Orlando, Florida, a consulting firm that applies training principles developed in sports to business executives.

GREG LOUGANIS is a former diver who won double gold medals in back-to-back Olympic Games. Later he revealed to the public that he was both gay and HIV-positive and became an advocate for human rights. He now mentors top U.S. divers.

DANIEL McGINN is a senior editor at *Harvard Business Review,* and the author of *Psyched Up: How the Science of Mental Preparation Can Help You Succeed* (Portfolio, 2017). Follow him on Twitter @danmcginn.

ADRIAN MOORHOUSE is Managing Director of Lane4, a performance development consultancy.

BILL PARCELLS is a former head coach of four professional football teams: the New York Giants (1983–1990), the New England Patriots (1993–1997), the New York Jets (1997–1999), and the Dallas Cowboys (2003–2006). He was voted into the Pro Football Hall of Fame in 2013.

MATT ROGAN is a board director of Lane4 and the European Sponsorship Association.

TONY SCHWARTZ is the president and CEO of The Energy Project and the author of *Be Excellent at Anything*. Become a fan of The Energy Project on Facebook and connect with Tony on Twitter @TonySchwartz and @Energy_Project.

BILL TAYLOR is the cofounder of *Fast Company* and the author, most recently, of *Simply Brilliant: How Great Organizations Do Ordinary Things in Extraordinary Ways*. Learn more at williamctaylor.com.

MELANIE WHELAN is the CEO of SoulCycle.

Index

Invaluable insights
always at your fingertips

With an All-Access subscription to
Harvard Business Review, you'll get
so much more than a magazine.

Exclusive online content and tools
you can put to use today

My Library, your personal workspace for sharing,
saving, and organizing HBR.org articles and tools

Unlimited access to more than 4,000 articles in the
Harvard Business Review archive

Subscribe today at hbr.org/subnow

The most important management ideas all in one place.

We hope you enjoyed this book from *Harvard Business Review*. Now you can get even more with HBR's 10 Must Reads Boxed Set. From books on leadership and strategy to managing yourself and others, this 6-book collection delivers articles on the most essential business topics to help you succeed.

HBR's 10 Must Reads Series

The definitive collection of ideas and best practices on our most sought-after topics from the best minds in business.

- Change Management
- Collaboration
- Communication
- Emotional Intelligence
- Innovation
- Leadership
- Making Smart Decisions

- Managing Across Cultures
- Managing People
- Managing Yourself
- Strategic Marketing
- Strategy
- Teams
- The Essentials

hbr.org/mustreads

Buy for your team, clients, or event.
Visit hbr.org/bulksales for quantity discount rates.